SCUBA:
A Practical Guide for the New Diver

By
James A. Lapenta
SEI Diving Instructor, CMAS 2 Star Instructor

With an Introduction by Bernie Chowdhury
Author of "The Last Dive"

Edited by Elizabeth Babcock, MSW, LCSW
Illustrated by Casey A. Peel

Disclaimers

This book is not a manual to teach you how to SCUBA dive. That process requires training from a competent instructor in an organized class. No guarantee of safety without that training is stated or implied in any way. The opinions expressed herein are those of the author and do not necessarily reflect those of any other individual or entity, including businesses and training agencies. For information on training with the author, visit www.udmaquatics.com.

The illustrations are representative of individuals, situations, and equipment in general, and not of any one specific person or item. Photos, where used, are of the author's own personal equipment or are used with permission of the manufacturer and are noted as such. No photo should be interpreted as an endorsement of the brand shown.

First Edition published 2011, by the author.

Dedication

Deciding who to dedicate this work to was a difficult matter. Many contributed to the thoughts contained herein. None of this would have come about if I had not taken up SCUBA diving in the first place. My initial inspiration for taking up diving came from Lloyd Bridges (Mike Nelson on Sea Hunt) and Jacques Cousteau with his Undersea World television series in the '60s. It took nearly 35 years for me to get my initial certification after watching them, but they played a huge part in the decision. Thanks.

Once that decision was made, it was the support and encouragement of my late wife, Denise Lynne Churney, which not only saw me through my initial Open Water Class but made it possible for me to become an instructor. Few would have sacrificed what she did to see me through the whole process. For that I, and hopefully many others, will be eternally grateful. Rest in Peace.

This still would not have come to fruition without the support and help of my editor and friend, Elizabeth Babcock. Her guidance in matters of writing and composition are why you will not be tearing your hair out trying to read this work. If not for her, this would likely be a jumble of words in some vague semblance of order, still in a file on my computer. Any diver whose enjoyment of this sport is made greater or whose safety is increased, and any life that may be saved, is due as much to her efforts in this as it is to my words. She has made the words flow and make sense in a way I could not. Love you. Thank you for everything.

To my children, Josh and Katie, for just being you. To my grandfather, Dominic for teaching me to swim. To Casey Peel, for agreeing to do the illustrations in this book.

Divers who lost their lives were the reason this was started. Their deaths, detailed later in this book, were probably preventable. I had to write this if there was *any* chance that some of my words might prevent some future fatalities from occurring.

Finally, to all who desire to see first-hand what is under the surface of the water on SCUBA.

This is for you.

Introduction

James Lapenta's SCUBA: A Practical Guide for the New Diver is a trove of vital information for the new and aspiring diver, as well as for the more experienced. New divers may be surprised to learn that not all instructors and dive shops have the same focus – or strengths. The use of specific questions (listed in the pertinent sections) that the diver can direct at a potential instructor or dive shop should prove insightful. It should also help the diver to focus on what they themselves may want from their diving education and experiences and how to best achieve that.

As James rightfully points out, proper buoyancy skills are critical. Without those skills divers are not just frustrated and uncomfortable in the water, but they are a danger to themselves, to others, and to their environment. Typically, proper buoyancy takes the most time to master. When deciding which instructor to choose, a diver would do well to focus on how much time will be devoted in class to teaching buoyancy skills, and what sorts of skills are employed.

Unfortunately, the high price of renting time at a swimming pool often means that these critical skills -- and the time to develop them -- are given short shrift in many classes. With the trend to ever shorter diving courses, a potential diving student may think they're getting a good deal and that spending less time in a scuba class is a good idea. The reality is that a person only gets comfortable and learns to master diving skills through quality time spent underwater.

This Guide raises the very important notion of finding an appropriate mentor. High-quality underwater time -- with either a skilled, attentive, patient instructor or with an experienced diver- is the key for anyone wishing to grow in the sport. Professionals, such as Diving Instructors, Assistant Instructors and Dive Masters, are all very important in teaching the nuances of scuba diving. However, experienced divers and boat captains can also provide guidance. Finding a dive club or forming a casual group for camaraderie, adventure, to share knowledge and dive stories is an important part of maintaining interest in diving and realizing a lot of pleasure from it. James points out how and where one can reach out and find others to share the sport, and also to mentor the up-and-coming diver.

This Guide should serve divers well, not only immediately, but also in the future; it has been designed to serve as a handy reference. Flipping through these pages between dive trips, dive classes, or in the off-season will undoubtedly give divers new thoughts to ponder and help steer their diving through many enjoyable years.

Plan well, dive safely.
Bernie Chowdhury
DAN, NAUI, PADI, TDI Instructor
Author – *The Last Dive*

Dive Industry Feedback on
SCUBA: A Practical Guide for the New Diver

"I have recently had the opportunity to read an advance copy of the new book by Jim Lapenta. This well-written new book should be on every diver's book shelf. Potential divers, new divers, and experienced pros will benefit from the wise and thoughtful information. I have a good library of diving books, manuals, magazines, etc. My first purchase was the New Science of Skin and Scuba, some 40 years ago. This will be a go-to book and is a new standard. Thank you, Jim.

Great book."

Michael Brennan

President, Apollo Sports USA, INC.

"Finally, a book with a no-nonsense approach on the art of scuba diving. Real life examples are presented throughout the book, which help drive home the points of proper and improper techniques. This should be a must-read for anyone that is interested in getting involved in the sport. Jim has presented the basics of scuba diving in a clear, easy-to-understand format that is not only good for the new diver, but a good review for the seasoned one."

Capt. Gary

Conch Republic Divers

Master Scuba Diving Instructor with PADI and SSI

Staff Instructor with SDI/TDI

NSS Full Cave Diver

"It is obvious that you are passionate about our sport and the safety of not only your students, but all divers. I applaud you for that."

Dan Orr, President

Divers Alert Network (DAN)

"Thank you for the privilege of reading your new book. While the "why" of diving hasn't really changed, the reality is the "how" has undergone many dramatic changes in the last couple decades. Not only has instructional technique changed, but consumer expectations have radically shifted. This shift has left many in the dive instruction field and our students "not getting a view of the ocean for the cove." Your book is a very down-to-earth and honest look at where we are and how new divers can find their way. I will recommend the book to divers new and old and more importantly, to instructors and dive shops."

Chris Richardson

NAUI 17055 Technical and Recreational Course Director

ACUC #1049EA Advanced Instructor

TDI, ERDI and SDI Instructor #4587

PADI MSDT 157937

Foreword

I am writing this in order to impress on new divers just what this activity called SCUBA diving is. While it is indeed a fun, relaxing, educational, interesting, and -- if approached properly -- safe activity, it is nonetheless a sport that has risks. SCUBA diving is in fact an extreme sport that can injure or even kill very quickly, and in some very nasty ways. What we are doing is entering an alien environment that is normally hostile to human life. We cannot breathe in water without some kind of mechanical assistance. In this case, we use a steel or aluminum high pressure cylinder, a means of reducing that pressure to a level that we can safely breathe (i.e., a regulator), and a means of controlling our buoyancy.

We also need a mask to allow us to see, fins to help us propel ourselves through the water, and a few other items that are specific to different environments and conditions. These are all covered, or should be, in every Open Water (OW) class. All too often in today's society, however, people do not want to take the time to properly prepare and get the education to safely take on new tasks. Some agencies appear to have responded to this by developing training programs that turn out high numbers of certified divers in shorter time frames, necessitating the reduction of time spent on what I consider to be some necessary basic skills.

While this has resulted in great numbers of new divers entering the water, it has not resulted in many of those divers staying in the water. New divers are often given just enough training to enable them to dive in the most benign conditions under close supervision. Even then, there are still those who find out their initial training was just not adequate. It is at this point that they either make the decision to get more training or they leave the sport. The latter happens all too often. The former, when it does happen, does not always occur for the right reasons. Students should return to training to expand their diving and learn new skills; they should not have to return for new training just to be able to enjoy the sport safely.

To require students to come back for basic information is something I find very troubling, and in some cases, has actually cost divers their lives. A lack of rescue instruction has resulted in a number of diver deaths when buddies did not know how to drop weights, support a diver at the surface, or even stay in contact with their buddy. This is another area frequently talked about, but all too often not actually put into practice. The concept of always diving with a buddy and just what that means in the "real world" is often given too little attention. Unfortunately, it is impossible to foresee every conceivable situation that can arise, but there are many basic issues that can be covered. The following chapters will hopefully address much of what is being overlooked or delayed in many programs as they exist today.

It is my hope that this information also finds its way into the hands of those who have not yet begun the training process. I will include a chapter on how to select an instructor based on the quality of instruction and the content of the course. In some cases, these classes may cost more than the less comprehensive courses also available, but usually they do not. In fact, when you consider the additional skills and education gained from a more comprehensive course, you will find that you have received much more value for each dollar spent. In addition, you gain priceless benefits in the form of greater confidence, enjoyment, skills, and -- most importantly -- safety.

Enjoy.

James Lapenta

Table of Contents

Chapter One
Safe Diving Practices

SCUBA diving is a wonderful recreational activity with low risk of injury when well-trained divers practice it in a safe manner. When we think of safe diving practices, what comes to mind? Diving with a buddy at all times? Not going beyond your training and experience? Not diving in conditions that could be hazardous? Certainly these are some very good ones, but as we will see in this section, safe diving practices start before we even get near the water. Perhaps long before, when we have only just decided to take up the sport.

At some point you decided to take up SCUBA diving. Hopefully, when you made this decision you considered whether you could afford the time and money that it required, and whether it's something you really want. Since you're reading this, you most likely answered yes. Perhaps without realizing it, you already started using safe dive practices by getting the proper training from a qualified instructor, or at least doing the research to find one.

Continuing to have this mindset will go a long way towards making sure your diving is safe and enjoyable for years to come, as you commit yourself to never going beyond your training and experience. Will you be ready to do any dive you wish after your first class? Of course not, but by continuing to get experience and seeking out qualified instruction, the limitations as to where, when, and how you dive will be replaced by more and more options.

I also hope you have asked yourself if you are physically, emotionally, and mentally able to take on the challenges of SCUBA diving. Ideally, you've had a physical within the last year or two, are in relatively good shape, use tobacco or alcohol only in moderation or not at all, and try to get some type of exercise on a somewhat regular basis. This can be a demanding sport and being in good physical condition, although you don't need to be a super athlete, can help you avoid injury, reduce the amount of stress, and ensure that you have fun as well as be safe.

Diving can be mentally demanding, as well. You are about to undertake a sport where you will be using SCUBA gear to exist in what, to most people, is a hostile environment. Hostile, in that we cannot breathe water; we must rely on mechanical means to exist there. As such, we need to realize that at some point something could -- though it is rare -- go wrong and we will need to be able to get out of the situation in order to avoid being injured. For some, this can be a little much. The equipment can seem complicated at first and to some, confining. The mask may bring uneasiness in those who tend to be claustrophobic. Poor visibility can do the same. Such people may need to make adjustments as to type of gear and when they will or will not dive, or even consider another sport.

You may also need to consider whether any medications or treatments you are taking are contraindicative to diving. Anything that makes you sleepy, have trouble staying focused or concentrating, or is used to control a condition that may be less than friendly to diving may cause you to reconsider this activity as well. The use of recreational drugs and excessive alcohol consumption should be a clear indication that you and diving do not mix. Even moderate use of alcohol at the wrong time can present a serious risk to your safety. Smoking is another of those habits that nearly every physician will caution you against. I personally prefer not to train those who smoke, but I evaluate each person on a case-by-case basis. If a person cannot get through a two-hour class or pool session without a cigarette, it is best they find someone else to train them. Smoking has been proven to contribute to emphysema and other respiratory maladies. Any reduction of lung function or capacity can negatively affect you as a diver since efficient processing of the air you take in is critical.

Once all of these factors have been considered and you have concluded that there is nothing to preclude you from pursuing diving, we can go into the practices that relate directly to going into the water. We have already touched on training, but let's go into it with a little more detail. In a beginner class, you learned many new skills, practices, and a lot of information. You should also have learned how to use the gear you'll be wearing, how it functions, how to adjust and care for it, and how to inspect it. You should have learned how to enter and exit the water safely whether from shore or a boat, and to move through it efficiently and with seemingly little effort. You learned how to plan your dive. You also learned when to end a dive, or even not go into the water in the first place. There are times when the best plan involves saying no to diving that day.

Let's take a typical open water (OW) dive as an example. As a new diver, you'll need several things. You'll need gear, water, a plan as to what you are going to do and most importantly, a buddy or teammate. The last item mentioned is without a doubt, the most important to a new and even experienced diver. Safe diving necessitates that we don't take chances. Diving with a buddy ensures that there is someone there to assist us with planning the dive, gearing up, perhaps entering and exiting the water, and being able to handle any unforeseen situations that may arise. We will get into more detail on buddies in a later chapter.

You will hear of or perhaps even see divers going it alone or diving "solo." This is seldom discussed and I'm not going to go into detail here or debate whether it is right or wrong. Some consider it a form of technical diving in itself, and it should only be undertaken by those with the proper experience, training, equipment, and mindset. As a new Open Water Diver, you have none of these. So while you may see solo diving practiced, make no mistake, it is not for you.

Back to the typical OW dive. Before you even consider going in, you must first decide if the conditions are right for the dive. Do you have the training and experience for this dive? Does your buddy? If so, then you need to start preparing for it. How? By going through a kind of checklist, if you will. First of all, you've decided the dive is within your limits as far as training and experience goes. Now, do you have the gear for the dive? You will need to determine if you need anything beyond the basics: a mask, fins, snorkel, boots, and proper exposure protection are a start. You'll need a buoyancy compensation device (BCD or BC), regulator with an alternate air source (also called an octopus), necessary gauges or computer, weights, and of course, an air supply: your tank, sometimes called a cylinder.

You'll also need to be familiar with how these pieces of gear function. Now, in order to do the dive safely, do you need anything else? Will you need a reel or line? A light? Sometimes even on daylight dives, a light is nice for looking under things and can be used for signaling. Do you need a compass? To my way of thinking, compass use should be a core skill of the competent diver. We'll look at basic navigation skills later. Will you need some type of signaling device for underwater or on the surface? Will you need a cutting tool? Here's a hint: if you dive where people fish, it's a good idea to have a small knife or EMT shears with you.

Now that you've determined you have everything you need, before you go into the water, where are you? Is there help available on shore? Is there EMS service available should an accident occur, and do you know how to contact them? This is not to put a damper on your day of fun; these are things you should consider to make your diving safe. Now that all of these items are checked and okay, it's time to get in the water! But wait... no it's not! Now you have to decide what kind of dive you are going to do. Is there a purpose for the dive or is it just to have fun and relax, which in itself is a very good purpose for diving. Let's say that it's a fun dive from shore to just relax and maybe work on a few skills, which by the way you should try to do on every dive. You need to have a plan before you even think about getting in.

How long is the dive going to last? When will you end it? Where will you be going and how will you get there? How long the dive will last depends on a number of factors: how much air you have, how deep you will be going, the water temperature, and how long you want the dive to last. Once you've answered these questions, the next step is to plan the dive. At this point, you'll start the formal planning with either the dive tables you learned to use in your OW class, or by using your computer if predive planning is one of its functions. Even if you use your computer, it's a good idea to also plan the dive using tables as a backup in the event your computer fails due to dead batteries, flooding, or for any other reason. You and your buddy will also agree upon a course, what you'll do in the event you get separated or one of you has a problem, and what signals you'll use to communicate. You may also decide to do a surface swim to the area you wish to dive and then descend, or just go the whole way underwater. All of this is necessary to keep potential surprises to a minimum. Generally, the fewer surprises, the safer the dive is.

Safe diving practices dictate that once you plan your dive, you dive your plan. Major variations in the dive plan once you're underwater should only occur in exceptional circumstances. Minor ones are to be expected, perhaps due to changing currents, visibility being better or worse than expected, water colder or warmer, or perhaps a new feature has been added to the site and requires a little more time. All is well as long as the overall plan is followed and the changes are agreed upon by all parties. However, any questions or doubts as to the change overrule that change. If your buddy does not want to change the plan, then you have two choices: continue on the original plan or end the dive. Remember that any diver may end a dive at any time, with no explanation necessary. Once the decision is made to end a dive, it ends. Period!

Now that you have a plan agreed upon by all, it's time to gear up and enter the water. By now you should have determined the safest entry and exit, agreed upon it, and be ready to go. Next thing is to gear up, one of many circumstances in which your buddy can come in very handy. Gear can be heavy, and having someone help you with putting it on makes it easier while avoiding unnecessary strain and injury. Have your buddy help lift and hold your tank/BC/regulator assembly while you put it on. Then do the same for your buddy. Next, go over each other's gear looking for loose hoses, clips, releases, and other things that may be dangling or not properly fastened or secured. In the event a problem occurs and you or your buddy needs to remove the other's gear, it is necessary that you be familiar with each other's setup. Check to be sure the air is fully on and that the power inflator is connected and works; your buddy will then do the same for you. The pre-dive or buddy check is perhaps one of the biggest safety precautions you can undertake. An extra set of eyes may prevent a problem from occurring that could otherwise result in serious consequences. You'll then verify each other's air supply, be sure it's on, and that your regulators are functioning as they should. You'll also check to be sure you each have your weight system on, properly placed, and fastened. It is good practice to actually remove and replace your buddy's weights before entering the water, so you know exactly how the release mechanism functions.

Being properly weighted goes a long way towards diving safely. Too much weight can cause overexertion, while too little can leave you unable to control your ascent; the latter risk is also an issue if you lose weights while diving because they were not properly secured. Safe diving practices dictate that you determine the proper amount of weight you'll be using either through experience or by doing a buoyancy or weight check at the beginning of your dive. It is also a good idea that once you've determined this, you make a record of it for future reference. We will look at how to adjust for proper weighting and trim later, in Chapter Two.

Now you should be ready to don your mask and fins, and begin your dive. The first thing you'll do when you enter the water is to do a bubble check to be sure there are no leaks in your air supply/regulator assembly and your BC. Satisfied that everything is a go, you'll note the time, your air pressure, your buddy's air pressure, and begin the dive. If everything goes according to plan, you'll enjoy a safe, fun, and perhaps even exciting experience.

This is just one example of a typical OW dive using safe diving practices. There are many others and the more you dive, the more you will need to adjust to varying conditions, new gear, and even new buddies. As long as the basic practices are followed, each dive should result in more enjoyment, a greater appreciation for the underwater world, and you becoming a better diver. To summarize:

1. Determine that diving is what you want to do.

2. Make sure you are in good physical, mental, and emotional health. Be sure there are no reasons that would indicate you are not suited for diving.

3. Be sure that you can devote the time necessary for proper training and instruction.

4. Get your training from a quality instructor.

5. Once trained, never dive beyond your training and experience.

6. Should you wish to extend your dive range, get the proper instruction and experience to do so.

7. Plan your dives and dive your plans.

8. Be sure you have the necessary gear and that it's in good condition.

9. Avoid overhead environments until trained and equipped to enter.

10. Dive with a buddy or teammate at all times. Be familiar with your buddy's gear and skills. Check each other's equipment while gearing up and make any necessary fixes before you get in the water.

11. Don't let anyone talk you into taking shortcuts in training or into doing dives you may have doubts about. This is a biggie, because some dive operations have a reputation for taking Open Water divers deeper than they should go, into areas they are not trained for, and on dives that are beyond the skills and abilities of some members of the dive group. Don't let peer pressure put you in a situation that you are not ready for. Your mom told you this when she said, "If Joey Smith jumped off a cliff, would you do it, too?"

12. Never forget that at any time, for any reason, you may end a dive without going into a long explanation as to why. A

simple, "It did not feel right to me," is more than sufficient reason, but if you're not confident in saying that, try, "I couldn't equalize," or, "My ears started bothering me." These reasons are usually accepted by others without question.

These are the basics. As you progress in your diving you will need to add to them. Deeper dives, different environments, or an upgrade of equipment may require you to add more, but at no time should you do less. Your confidence will increase as you gain experience, get more certifications, and dive different places. Don't let any of these things make you complacent, however. Getting so relaxed and confident that you start taking shortcuts or forgetting the basics altogether could have serious, potentially lethal consequences. That's a strong statement which is not meant to scare you, but to reinforce what was stated at the beginning of this article: SCUBA is a fun, exciting, and safe activity as long as you follow the rules. The fact remains that you are entering an environment that is hostile to human life without life-support gear. It is exciting, wonderful, enchanting, new, and different, but it's been said that the sea is a harsh mistress. Respect her and treat her kindly and she'll show you wonders you could previously only dream of. Lose that respect, ignore your training, or fail to use safe diving practices, however, and she may turn and bite you. Perhaps even cost you your life.

It is essential for Open Water students to keep these ideas in mind so that they can conduct safe dives independently. The message too often is that SCUBA diving is all fun, excitement, and relaxation. To a large degree it is, but there are essential issues that need to be considered before we jump into that fun, exciting, and relaxing environment. We will look at a number of these issues in the following chapters. It is my sincere hope that this work will not only make you a safer diver but also one who is more informed. Safety cannot be overemphasized when it comes to SCUBA diving. Some of the ideas in the following pages may seem restrictive or even a bit over the top, based on some training programs and the way they are conducted today. The only intent here is to keep you from getting hurt, or worse.

This work was inspired by a project in which I evaluated a number of accidents that resulted in fatalities among new and newer divers. The results were sobering. In each case, the cause of the incidents I investigated could be traced directly back to a lack of training or inadequate reinforcement of that training. During this process, my late wife observed the disturbing effect these findings had on me. She made me promise to never let an unprepared diver in the water with my name on their certification card. I will keep that promise as long as I teach people to enter the world beneath the waves.

©2007 James A Lapenta – Rush hour, Molasses Reef Key largo

NOTES

Chapter Two
Basic Skills

There are many different ideas about what constitutes basic skills when it comes to SCUBA diving. Everyone agrees that equalizing, mask clearing, regulator retrieval, and weight system remove/replace are basic skills that every diver should possess. Some consider equipment removal and replacement, non-silting kicks, and knowing one's air consumption rates to be among those basic skills that even a new diver should have. Still others feel that new divers should know how to get off and on a boat, find their way underwater, and be able to assist or even rescue another diver. What is your idea of basic skills? I know what mine is; it is all of the above, plus a bit more. As a diver and as an instructor, I have a personal opinion of what basic skills a diver should possess. At the minimum, a diver should have all of the skills that would permit me to allow them to dive with someone I cared about (son, daughter, wife, etc.) without me or another professional in the water. I would also expect them to have the skills and good judgment to be able to stay out of trouble and to assist another diver as needed.

Unfortunately, many divers appear to have -- at best -- the skills to barely survive a dive, let alone enjoy it and be able to assist a buddy. They have been trained with the idea that they will be diving with a divemaster (DM) or guide, and therefore need only minimum self-sufficiency. The fact is, and will be discussed in the chapter on diving with a buddy, that the only person you should be completely reliant on when you dive is yourself. For this reason the basic skills I feel are necessary for OW divers are those which allow you to fulfill the requirements as stated by the Recreational SCUBA Training Council (RSTC).

The stated goal of all members of the council is to produce OW divers who are capable upon receiving their certification card to plan, execute, and safely return from a dive in conditions equal to or better than those in which they trained. You should be able to do this with a buddy of equal skill and training, and no dive professional present. As anyone who has spent any amount of time around popular training sites or on dive boats can attest, this is not what is going on. New divers will see other new divers who cannot assemble their own gear, do not do buddy checks, allow the DM or guide to plan their dives without question, and have really poor skills in the water. They are not able to hold trim or control their buoyancy, appear to be dog paddling, demonstrate poor or even non-existent buddy skills, and are in some cases an accident waiting to happen.

They can clear their mask, recover their regulator, and remove and replace their weights under ideal conditions. But put them under a little stress or in a situation where the diver needs to handle two or more issues at the same time, and they are unable to do so. Basic skills are reinforced mainly through experience and practice, preferably done before diving in open water. What this means is that these skills should be given sufficient attention and time in confined water and under different task loads. By this, I mean they should be combined with other, more complex skills designed to challenge the student while increasing their confidence and problem solving ability. Then, when the student's mask gets kicked and dislodged by another diver, for example, they do not have a problem. They simply continue to swim, adjust and clear, or remove and replace the mask instead of panicking.

In addition, newly certified divers should be able to swim in a horizontal position and not be kicking the reef or stirring up excess amounts of silt. You should know where your buddy is at all times, and be in position to assist that buddy should the need arise. As such, it is my opinion that the following skills should be possessed by every diver and so should be added to the basics that are taught in many courses today.

NOTES

Buoyancy Control and Trim

These two skills are not something to be overlooked or delayed. Good buoyancy control and trim are the foundation of a skilled and -- more importantly -- safe diver. Not being able to set, adjust, and control one's buoyancy results in increased air consumption, excess stress, and can present the very real danger of an uncontrolled ascent or descent.

Now we need to look at just what buoyancy is. What appears to be a complex or difficult skill truly is not, if approached and taught in the correct way at the correct time. During the swimming, snorkeling, and skin diving portion of the training course we also work on mask remove/replace, snorkel clear (which is just what clearing a regulator is), and basic propulsion techniques. A good class will also begin to deal with equalization issues during the skin diving instruction. If this is done before actually using SCUBA, it allows the instructor to introduce buoyancy control as the first skill on SCUBA. It begins with properly weighting students instead of giving them amounts of weight that plant them on the bottom.

Doing a proper weight check is not difficult, but it does take a little time. There are numerous formulas used by different agencies and instructors for initial weighting. My usual method is to take 5% of the student's body weight in just a swim suit and start there. I also prefer to use weight belts even with a weight-integrated BC, using the integrated pockets or the pockets of the BC itself to add weight. We then start in the usual manner by having students move into deeper water so that they cannot stand, asking them to take a full breath from the regulator, hold it, and dump all the air from their BCs. Everyone should float at approximately eye-level. At this point, they are asked to exhale and should begin to slowly descend. If not, we will add weight in two-pound increments for anyone who needs it until they do. If anyone sinks like a rock I will not stop there, because divers should be able to descend in a controlled manner, and sinking like a stone is not controlled. I will stop the descent of any over-weighted student and remove two pounds, repeating the process until the proper weight is determined.

Once proper weighting has been roughly established, we will move back into shallow water and work on equalizing and descending in a horizontal position. In this way, we introduce the idea of trim while working on buoyancy. Trim is used to describe the orientation of a diver; the ideal orientation is horizontal because this presents the least amount of drag on the diver. Reduced drag results in less resistance so propulsion is more effective; because less work is required to move through the water, air consumption is reduced. We will discuss more factors affecting trim later in this chapter, but let's focus on buoyancy right now.

Once we have descended to the bottom of the pool in the shallow end, we relax and just breathe. Allowing a student to relax and get used to the idea of breathing underwater is often overlooked, but when included in training, primes students for more timely discovery of what buoyancy control really is. It is not magic, it is not complex, and it is not beyond the understanding or capabilities of the average OW student. What buoyancy control really amounts to is adding and subtracting small amounts of air from a flexible container. That container can be the BC, the lungs, or if using one in later training, a dry suit. In any case, when approached slowly and in a logical manner, buoyancy control is one of the simpler skills. That adding and subtracting of air begins by using the BC inflator, which should be explained in the classroom equipment lecture before students enter the water on SCUBA. Having practiced with it on the surface before descending, it is now time for students to try it underwater.

I will demonstrate the use of the inflator/deflator mechanism and then ask students to do so. The important thing about this is to clearly demonstrate and be sure students understand the importance of using *small* bursts of air and releasing it the same way. Of equal importance is to be sure they understand the need to maintain a steady, even breathing pattern. Once students have experimented with this BC operation for a few minutes, it is time to integrate that with breathing and do the fin pivot exercise.

16

While manipulating the inflator, students will also be instructed to alter their breathing patterns at different points. From slow, deep inhalations and exhalations to ones done just a bit faster, I encourage them to experiment. This allows them to see the effect breathing has on buoyancy and trim, and to note that *it takes time for buoyancy changes to become evident*. For example, a diver takes in a long, deep breath, increasing the volume of air in the lungs. That greater airspace will cause the diver's body to slowly begin to rise, but the full effect will not be evident until the diver is actually in the act of beginning to exhale. Likewise, as the air volume is decreased through exhaling, the diver will lose "lift," but this effect will also happen on a several- second delay. With practice, students learn to maintain a steady rhythm so that the effects actually offset each other and the desired depth is maintained. The inflator is used less and less as students learn to manage lung volume through the use of deeper or shallower breaths coupled with slower or faster rates of respiration.

As we approach a coral head or large rock that we do not want to go around, we inhale just a bit more and begin to rise. We exhale near the top and as we pass over it, we exhale just a bit longer. The result is a slow, controlled, effortless glide over the object followed by a slow, easy descent on the other side, and we never even had to think about using the power inflator. This takes practice but it can be done on nearly every dive at one point or another. If you have the chance, go to the pool and experiment with altering your breathing patterns. Try them in the fin pivot position. Do some "push-ups" using only your lung volume. Then swim and try the same exercises. Chances are if you've not done much of this before and now begin to work on it, you'll be amazed at the amount of control you have. A caution though – *at no time should you hold your breath!* All you want to do is alter your breathing pattern, not stop it. Start out with small changes and see how each one affects your buoyancy and trim. Don't be afraid to also work with your weighting while doing this. You may find that the more you control your breathing, the less weight you will need.

Once students have done this and are comfortable with it, the time has come to show them how to be neutral while horizontal.

The pool that I use has three different levels separated with clear steps, as seen in the next diagram.

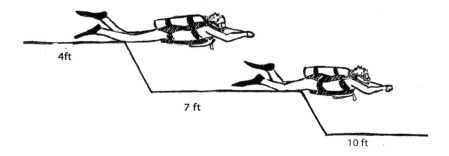

4ft

7 ft

10 ft

I have the students move as buddy pairs so that their torsos are out over the seven foot level with their legs on the four foot level. I then have them let the air out of their BCs so that they begin to drop; for now, it is okay if they put their hand out as they do this. Once they have stabilized, I have them add air until they are horizontal and relaxed. At this point, we begin basic skills starting with clearing a mask. If this goes well, I have them move further out so that just their knees are resting on the upper level as they do more practice with the inflator. Once stable and horizontal, I have them perform a mask remove/replace and a regulator remove/replace. Following successful completion of these skills, I move them out until just their fin tips are on the step. We will again do a mask remove/replace, regulator recovery using the sweep method, and a weight belt remove/replace. We will then move down a level and repeat the skills.

With a few basic skills now successfully practiced at two different depths, it is now time for students to swim around neutrally and just relax. During the swim they will again be asked to clear and then remove/replace the mask, recover the regulator, and remove/replace the weight belt. After completing these exercises, students should be given more time to just swim and relax. Every session in the pool from this point on will begin with doing basic skills while neutral and horizontal, with additional exercises and task loading scenarios being added during subsequent sessions. All new skills will be based on these initial exercises involving adding and subtracting small amounts of air from a flexible container or

18

containers -- complex tasks performed while performing a relatively simple one.

Next, students will begin to refine the position in which they perform these tasks. They will begin to work on their trim.

©2007 James A Lapenta – Barracuda (masters of trim), Key Largo

NOTES

Basic Trim

Trim refers to the positioning of the body while moving underwater; the horizontal position is generally the best one for diving. When a diver is horizontal (in trim) there is less drag on the body. Swimming is more efficient, less energy is required, less air is used, and it is better for the environment. When in trim, the diver is less likely to tear up the bottom, stir up silt, disturb sea life, or damage coral.

Trim is accomplished through body positioning, weighting, and equipment configuration. At the very least, divers should be able to swim along a reef or lake bottom without damaging it or stirring up silt behind them. There are kicking techniques that reduce the likelihood of this, but their effectiveness depends on the diver being horizontal in the water. ***This is another reason to get divers off their knees during training.*** Once a proper weight check has been done and students have had some practice using the inflator, it is also time to reinforce the idea that divers do not dive on their knees. There are no platforms in the ocean or in many freshwater sites, so it is best to avoid making students dependent on the kneeling position for comfortable practice of skills.

When instructors are demonstrating skills for students in midwater and in a horizontal position, we are also demonstrating trim. When we have students swimming around and performing basic skills, we should also be correcting their position in the water. This can be done by occasionally stopping students and indicating whether they need to be more head up, head down, or use their legs differently depending on what kick is being practiced. We can give students tips on how to arch their backs or use their hands out in front of them to help with horizontal positioning if necessary. In subsequent sessions, we can also move weights around or adjust the height of the tank in the BC to help with getting horizontal.

No matter what method we use, it is imperative that our students understand the importance of maintaining buoyancy and trim while performing all the basic skills. It is also necessary at this point to stress that this is just the beginning when it comes to trim. As divers gain experience and dive in different locations, they may need to change exposure protection, size of the tank they use, or even what accessories they must carry. All of these variables have the potential to affect trim and require adjustments to maintain it. Students must be taught to expect that maintaining trim becomes easier over time, but will always require regular practice. Competent divers should be able to take any BC, properly weight themselves, and achieve horizontal trim within a few minutes.

Open Water students are likely to hear that buoyancy and trim are skills that new divers can achieve down the road, and that the most important thing to start is to just dive and have fun. The truth is that buoyancy and trim are not impossible or even difficult for most students. With proper training and a little effort, both of these are completely within the capabilities of divers right out of the basic Open Water class. Students who master these skills early will enjoy their diving much more and much sooner than those who don't.

With buoyancy and trim now properly introduced, we need to go back and look more at weighting. Proper weighting is sometimes overlooked in the education of Open Water students. Students often experience what I call "planting," the practice of weighting students so they stay stuck or "planted" on the bottom. Stabilizing students in this manner may allow instructors to get students through the basic requirements of a course more quickly, but at the expense of spending a bit more time to establish good fundamental skills in those students.

This can clearly expedite training, but it can also result in certified divers who know barely enough to get by and will likely feel an immediate need for additional training. The problem is that many times, they do not come back. Sometimes the lack of comprehensive training results in a less than enjoyable experience the first time out and they do not dive again.

None of this has to happen. Proper buoyancy, trim, and proper weighting should be the fundamental basis for all SCUBA training. From the basic Open Water class through the professional ranks, the mark of an accomplished and competent diver is positional control in the water. To increase this control, the basics need to begin immediately, beginning the first time the diver descends underwater on SCUBA.

Other Skills

Now that we have established that buoyancy and trim are indeed basic skills, let's look at other skills that should be in the toolbox of the new diver. Every certifying agency requires some level of demonstrated proficiency in mask remove/replace, regulator recovery, weight system remove/replace, and some form of BC remove/replace. While BC remove/replace is not required to be done in a horizontal position, the other skills should be easy to perform in this orientation for the properly trained diver. The OW diver who must get vertical to do any of these is perhaps not ready to be out of the pool. Again, there are no platforms in the ocean and kneeling on the reef is a big no-no.

At one time, there were a number of additional skills included in every basic Open Water class, but many of these have been eliminated or moved to other courses. The reasons given are that these skills are too difficult for new divers, take too much time, or are not necessary at the basic level. A reality of these changes however, is that a given skill level now costs much more for a diver to attain than it used to. And that's only when divers come back – remember that they often don't. A diver may have a frightening experience or realize that he or she lacks sufficient skills for this sport and give up out of frustration. Some simply have so much difficulty that any enjoyment they might have gotten out of diving is gone. Whatever the reason, they do not come back for more training and we all lose them from this sport.

Fortunately, increasing numbers of instructors are making an effort to develop training programs to maximize diver confidence and competence rather than just meeting minimum standards. Their courses contain all the information a diver needs to plan, execute, and safely return from a dive with a buddy of equal skill, with no dive professional present, and in conditions similar to or better than those in which the training occurred. Because new divers should have the ability to assist their buddies should a problem arise, these more comprehensive courses also include some basic rescue skills

A number of fatal accidents have occurred because the buddies lacked the knowledge and skills to assist each other. At least some of these lives could have been saved if OW training included (as it used to) the following skills: diver tows while removing gear and giving rescue breaths, bringing an unconscious diver up from depth, supporting a diver at the surface, and assisting a panicked diver at the surface. These skills have the potential to save a life and do not require extensive training for basic competence; they should be in every diver's toolbox. Knowing how to assist a fellow diver creates the confidence that results in a safer and more enjoyable experience. A rescue tow is not much different than the tired-diver tow that is taught in most classes, with the exception of the addition of removing gear while giving rescue breaths. This adds a new dimension to the task but not one that should not be beyond any diver's ability.

There has been some recent discussion as to the effectiveness of rescue breathing while in water. Some research seems to indicate that there is a definite benefit to this, but it is a skill that takes a great deal of practice to perform effectively when both divers are in deep water. Of more importance is the swift extraction of a non-breathing diver from the water. Removal of gear can save valuable time in getting the diver out of the water; lifting an unconscious diver from the water is made infinitely easier if the tank, weight belt, and BC have been removed. Towing an unconscious diver while only removing equipment is much easier than performing rescue breaths while towing the diver, and it gets the rescuer and victim to a position of stability in much less time.

Time is one of the most critical aspects of diver rescue. It is essential to use any available means to reduce the time between recovery of the victim and getting him or her to safety and professional medical attention. Time saved can mean the difference between a successful and unsuccessful outcome for the victim. There is a window of recovery that slowly closes as time passes and the more time that passes, the faster that window closes. At one time, rescue skills were included in every Open Water class; this is another unfortunate example of the kinds of core skills not addressed in most basic training today. There is also little if any mention of the use of good buddy skills for effectively assisting as a team; this may even be treated as an afterthought in many rescue classes. It is unlikely that divers who are skilled and practice good buddy skills will need to rescue each other. They may, however, encounter a less skilled diver who requires assistance that his own buddy is unable to give. Buddy skills in such situations make the rescue more effective, and also much safer for the rescuers.

©2007 James A Lapenta – Nurse Shark on the Benwood, Key Largo

Chapter Three
Buddy Skills

One of the most talked about, yet also most neglected, aspects of dive training is the buddy system. While the buddy system has been a part of recreational SCUBA diving for over 50 years, it is often given little more than lip service at the Open Water level. We'll often be at a dive site or on a dive boat with a group of people and on the surface it appears that there are buddy pairs or teams. They assist each other with gear, perhaps do a check, and enter the water. At this point, everything can start to break down as divers scatter in different directions at different speeds and depths, more closely resembling the results of pulling the trigger on a sawed-off shotgun than they do good dive buddies.

The question is why? Were buddy skills not covered in their training? The disturbing answer is often no. To be sure, buddy skills are discussed and promoted, but actual use is not effectively or sufficiently taught. To expand on this I now submit the following treatise, "The Failure of the Buddy System." This was developed in response to and as a result of my research on diver fatalities.

The Failure of the Buddy System

The incidents I analyzed all resulted in the deaths of divers who were either new to the sport, or who had been out of the water for an extended period. These incidents do not include all the deaths that occurred in the two year period I studied, but what they all have in common is that each fatality was likely preventable. In each case, the buddy system was not followed and as a result, divers died. My research suggests that these divers died because they ignored the buddy system, and that in many cases they were not properly trained in it to begin with. When we talk about using the buddy system, it is not about just being in the same ocean, lake, or quarry and being fairly close through most of the dive. However, this seems to be common practice for many new divers I have spoken to and whose comments I have read. From the time of their first OW class they have indeed talked about always diving with a buddy, but from their descriptions and my own observations, it is clear that many do not put it into practice.

©2008 James A.Lapenta – Buddy pair, Bonaire

The buddy system, properly utilized, results in two divers acting as one. They move together, swim together, ascend and descend at the same time and rate. Sounds simple, doesn't it? So why are so many new divers getting separated, lost, injured, and even dying? Is it training or lack thereof, lack of attention to details, neglecting the rules, or a combination of all of these? The buddy system is one of the most fundamental tenets of recreational diving. My research suggests that its breakdown goes straight back to the OW course and the instructor. Coupled with the reduction of standards by some agencies and increased pressure to turn out large numbers of divers, the buddy system and proper procedures for it are not getting the attention they need. As a result, divers are dying.

What are we talking about when we say proper buddy procedures? The concept of buddy diving is a holdover from the original YMCA Swimming program where it was always stressed that you should never swim alone. When the first national SCUBA training agency was established through the "Y," many of the swimming rules were carried over, including the buddy system. Swimmers were taught to stay together at all times and maintain a distance at which one could quickly and easily assist the other if necessary.

SCUBA training was established in the same vein, and the buddy system was one of the ideas that became universal throughout the development of programs, regardless of agency. What has happened since is that many programs have been shortened and many of the exercises and skills that encouraged proper buddy procedures have fallen by the wayside. For example, were you buddied up with someone in your very first pool session? Were you told that no matter what, you stay within arm's reach of your buddy at all times? At all times?

Students in pool sessions are often put in a line or semicircle around the instructor. The instructor demonstrates a skill and then the students each perform the skill, one at a time. When you did this, where was your buddy and what was he or she doing? In my class, the diver's buddy is always within arm's reach. When we descend, my rule is that buddy pairs descend at the same time and immediately establish eye contact. From then on, each never requires more than a turn of the head to know where the other is. Even when doing individual skills with me, I want buddies to be within reach of each other.

The buddy system should be introduced and emphasized from the first pool session. By the time you get to more complex skills, the buddy system should already be one of the building blocks of the rest of the training. From the number of accidents and the cases of simple buddy separation among new divers, it is clear that this is not the case. Even in poor visibility, there is really no excuse for buddies to become separated. Properly trained divers will do a number of things to avoid separation. Moving closer together, using a buddy line, linking arms, or taking hold of each other's hands or equipment can all be used.

27

A buddy team can even avoid separation in poor visibility environments by calling the dive and not risking an incident at all.

When a buddy team begins a dive plan, what's the first decision they should make before they enter the water after all other aspects have been considered? With my students, it's position. Who will be on which side? After that they are taught to decide on who is leading, who is navigating, and who will be monitoring depth and time. Then they need to decide who will control the rate of descent and ascent. Following this, they will determine who will set the pace of the swim. *Hopefully you know that it is always the slowest swimmer who sets the pace.* This has become an issue in many areas as divers rely on a divemaster or guide to set the pace. These guides are often not in a position to even see everyone in the group, let alone judge the speed of each diver in the group.

Another problem in the buddy system is revealed when dive guides are looked at as everyone's buddy. The fact is that unless specifically contracted to be so, they are *no* one's buddy. All divers remain responsible for themselves and their buddies on every dive, without exception. Decreasing awareness of this principle seems to correlate with the shorter OW programs being offered by some agencies. Too many divers do not even know how to be proper buddies, let alone dive as a team. Let's take a look at some events where this is demonstrated, with tragic results. The following incident happened on a guided dive in Grand Cayman in 2008.

A recently certified 58 year old man and his fiancée were on a dive with five other divers and a dive guide. This was the man's second dive after his checkouts. The first mistake on this particular dive was that it occurred at all. The plan was for a 100 foot wall dive on a spot with a hard bottom at roughly several hundred feet. All the divers were following the guide except for two women who elected to stay at 60 feet while the others followed the guide. What happened is not totally clear because at some point, the victim became separated from the group descending to the planned depth. One of the women who stayed at 60 feet was the victim's fiancée and should have been his buddy. She stated that the buddy system was talked about, but did not feel it had been emphasized in their OW class. Had it been, her fiancé may have elected to stay with her and would likely still be alive.

In any event, he did not stay with his buddy and after all was said and done, his computer indicated he had descended to 342 feet and made a two minute ascent from 302 feet. This dive is burned in my mind as a prime example of the buddy system gone as wrong as can be, in part because I heard about it directly from the other woman on the dive who remained at 60 feet, who later came to me from out-of-state for additional training because of the emphasis I put on buddy skills. First of all, none of the divers on this trip should have been on a 100 foot wall dive at all. The dive occurred even though the guide knew he had two newly certified divers, a 16 year old boy who had not been diving recently, a couple who was not going to be together because the wife had a personal limit of 60 feet that she was comfortable with, and another couple who also expressed concern about the depth. The woman I later taught stated that the guide assured them this was going to be okay and that he did it all the time -- this is frightening in itself. Had proper buddy procedures been followed, a number of different scenarios could have occurred, any one of which would likely have prevented the fatality:

1. The dive might not have occurred at all.

2. The dive site could have been changed.

3. The buddy pairs could have been set and the depth adjusted for the dive.

4. The buddy pairs could have exercised good, independent judgment and refused to do the dive.

5. The buddy pairs could have insisted that the guide change the planned depth.

None of these things happened, and a tragedy occurred. The death of this man clearly goes back to the initial instruction and the failure of that instruction to instill good judgment, insist on good buddy procedures, and clearly state the limits for OW divers and the reasons for them.

The next incident I'd like to analyze involved a woman who lived less than 15 minutes from me. She was a newly certified diver who was diving in waters off of Lauderdale by the Sea in Florida in 2009. The dive site, by all accounts, is a popular place for new divers as the conditions are usually fairly benign. For whatever reason, this woman and her husband were doing an early morning dive and though OW certified, were not what one would call highly experienced divers. In fact, this was one of their first dives as a buddy pair on their own. At some point, they elected to end the dive and began to swim for shore. The husband stated that he thought his wife was right behind him.

We will never know why they were not swimming together and most likely the husband may not be able to say why. But had it been reinforced in their OW classes to always stay together, she may not have fallen behind. By his account, he was swimming in, turned to see where she was, and realized he could not see her. Not having the autopsy results, I cannot say what happened, but if she was having any type of difficulty he may have been able to assist her. As a result he was not able to locate her, much less assist her. She died and was found by two other divers who had also been in the water. If this couple had been using proper buddy protocol, they would not have been separated. These were newly certified divers; had proper buddy procedures been emphasized during their training, we can say with some confidence that they likely would have paid attention to it. Personally, I will not issue a card to students who display a tendency to deviate from proper procedures.

The next incident we'll review involved a father and son who were diving off of La Jolla Shores in California. They were on their first dive after certification and the father ran out of air... at 150 feet! This was a *planned* depth. The two began to ascend while sharing air and became separated. The son ran out of air at 40 feet and finished the ascent as a Controlled Emergency Swimming Ascent (CESA). The father was located eight hours later by a Remotely Operated Vehicle (ROV) employed for the search. This incident clearly demonstrates the necessity for OW training to strongly emphasize not only good buddy skills but also good judgment and respect for diving within one's limits. These are points that are actually getting less attention as certification standards change, not more.

Another incident involved a couple who were diving out of Key Largo when they surfaced farther from the boat than planned and tried to swim for it. The man indicated they had been swimming for half an hour when he looked back and his buddy's head was underwater. He was struggling to keep her up when a Florida Fish and Wildlife boat picked them up. She did not survive. Had proper buddy procedures and good judgment been used, they would have gotten positively buoyant at the surface, deployed a safety sausage, and waited for the boat to pick them up. They may have waited a few minutes longer, but no one would be dead.

Two particularly disturbing deaths involved buddies who did not become separated but when the time came for one to render assistance, he could not, either due to panic or because *he did not know how*!

The first occurred off of McAbee Beach on Cannery Row when a 49 year old man surfaced and yelled for help. He was brought to shore and stopped breathing. He had not been diving in about three years but had no known medical issues. It was determined he had panicked after getting tangled in some kelp and shot to the surface. His "buddy" was in a state of shock and unable to be of any assistance.

The next incident occurred at Dutch Springs in eastern Pennsylvania. Two divers, a man and a woman, were diving when the woman began having difficulties. Reports indicate that her inflator had a malfunction and she panicked. She made it to the surface, only to disappear back under the water. As help arrived, her buddy was attempting to keep her from sinking back to the bottom by hanging onto her octopus hose four feet from the surface. She did not dump her weights and her buddy was unable to do it. She was resuscitated and taken to a hospital, where she lapsed into a coma before dying.

Absolutely none of these incidents had to happen. All of them could have been avoided by proper use of the buddy system, but here we come to the crux of the problem. Apparently, none of these divers was sufficiently versed in utilizing basic buddy skills. They also lacked basic rescue skills that used to be taught in every OW class, but which are now offered in only the more comprehensive OW classes. Proper buddy protocol absolutely demands that the divers not only know how to swim around together, but also how to provide assistance in an emergency.

This brings us to the point of this essay: How do we as divers and instructors develop good buddy skills? The answer is to start using them as early as possible. The best place to start is in the first pool session, during the swimming and snorkeling portion of the OW course. By pairing up students from the beginning, we demonstrate the importance of the buddy system. There are a number of ways to develop and practice good buddy skills. I emphasize all of the following in my OW course because I consider them essential:

Communication between the divers, both on the surface and underwater.

Position. From day one, divers should be buddied up and required to stay in position.

Buoyancy control should be introduced immediately, to facilitate position.

Horizontal positioning from the very beginning, for skills. Skills are actually easier to perform in a horizontal position.

Looking like divers. Divers who look like divers will think, act, and feel like divers.

Speed during descents, swims, and ascents. No matter what, the slowest diver sets the pace of all aspects of the dive.

Good judgment, demonstrated by choosing appropriate dive sites, equipment, dive buddies, and whether or not to do a given dive at all. These are all parts of being a good buddy.

Rescue skills. Even basic skills such as tows, bringing an unconscious diver to the surface, air shares, assisting a panicked diver at the surface, and knowing how to release each other's weights are skills that every Open Water Diver should have. Unfortunately, many OW programs no longer include them all.

Choosing the right buddy. This goes back to good judgment, but also includes other considerations such as size, strength, skill, training, attitude, and personality.

Personal responsibility. The best divers always maintain ultimate responsibility for their own safety and should not expect their buddies to "carry" them through any dive.

Having summarized these ten essential elements of strong buddy skills, we'll now expand on each one a bit further.

Communication

Establishing and developing good communication skills is essential to any endeavor involving two or more people. For dive buddies, this actually starts long before they enter the water; it begins when the decision to dive is made. This is when good dive buddies will begin to discuss a plan for the dive or dives, including choosing a site, discussing the dive, considering entry options, or deciding on a boat operator. Each of these tasks requires the divers to communicate effectively. At the site, you will agree on hand signals and possibly also written methods such as a slate or wetnotes. During the dive you will monitor air pressures, depths, times, and course. Not only will you monitor these items and more, you will effectively communicate them to each other. Failure to do so can lead to situations where the end result is anything from a minor inconvenience to a tragedy.

Position

The importance of position in true buddy diving cannot be underestimated or overemphasized. Good instructors will see that new divers are buddied up with each other whenever possible from day one. Buddies then stay in position throughout all pool sessions. Even when repeating skills demonstrated by the instructor, the diver's buddy will be within arm's reach at all times. I require my students to do this; when a student is asked to move forward to perform a skill, the buddy also moves forward.

Buoyancy Control

Good buoyancy control is another essential aspect of being a good buddy. This is why I introduce basic buoyancy control within the first 20 minutes of the second pool session, which is the first night on SCUBA. This happens after I have properly weighted students and shown them how to do the check, themselves. There is no reason to delay this critical aspect of diving.

Horizontal Positioning

Basic skills are easier to perform in a horizontal position and are more natural to the beginning diver. Having students descend to a kneeling position often results in them flailing around trying to maintain their balance, falling backwards or sideways. In some cases, this may result in them getting upset enough to panic. If we introduce buoyancy control by having students descend in a horizontal position in the beginning, with feet spread in a nice stable base, they do not feel out of control. This results in students whose confidence has already been increased by the method of instruction, and who are more open to further instruction in early skills like mask clearing, regulator retrieval, and weight belt remove/replace. When students are asked to clear a mask while kneeling, they may tend to look down or straight ahead and have to be reminded to look up. When horizontal, it is natural to look up to see the instructor, which facilitates the skill. Regulator retrieval is easier since the regulator tends to fall to the side *as it would on an actual dive*. Weight belts are much easier to doff and don while prone. My students first practice new skills with their knees on the "step" in the pool and their bodies neutrally buoyant in midwater while horizontal; they eventually progress to doing the skills while having no contact with the pool bottom. The result is that by the time we hit open water, I can ask students to perform the skills at any time during the dive and they do not need to settle to their knees in order to comply.

Looking like Divers

Divers who look like divers will think, act, and feel like divers. When we include the first four items in basic instruction, it results in students who look like divers: horizontal, together, and in good trim. As a result they feel like the divers they've seen. Students will remain within arm's reach of each other at all times, and I will remind them to buddy up if they begin to get too far apart. By the end of the third or fourth session, they are beginning to think and act like divers. They will instinctively get in position relative to their buddies when entering the pool. They will confidently assist each other with equipment checks and verify proper weighting. They will look to each other before entering the water. The more they look, think, and act like divers, the more they will feel like divers, and the more they can actively engage in the process of learning.

Speed -- Descents, Swims, and Ascents

A common factor in buddy separations is one diver who descends, swims, or ascends faster than the other. If divers in Open Water training are firmly convinced of the need to let the slowest diver set the pace, there is no need for separation to ever occur. Even in low visibility situations, divers who are descending, swimming, and ascending at the same rate can maintain contact and communication. When planning a dive, the strengths and limitations of each diver need to be taken into account. If one buddy has equalization issues, that buddy sets the rate of ascent and descent. If one is a slower swimmer, then that buddy sets the pace of the swim. During Open Water checkout dives it is imperative that not only do buddies stay in proper position, but that the pace of the swims is adjusted to these guidelines regarding speed. It is unacceptable for an instructor or divemaster to set a pace that leaves students struggling to keep up.

Good Judgment

Choosing dive sites, equipment, dive buddies, and whether or not to do a dive at all are part of being a good buddy, and developing these abilities should begin in the OW class. It falls to the instructor to impress upon students that all of these choices have safety implications and are not to be taken lightly. A diver will make an effort to research the proposed dive sites, choose the proper equipment, ask questions of potential dive buddies to see if they are compatible, and assess whether or not a dive is within the training and abilities of the team. This does not happen overnight or in one session. It should be impressed upon the diver that time, experience, and good training are the principle factors in developing good judgment. Another factor that should never be overlooked or minimized in importance is that little voice that comes from inside, the one that says, "This may not be a good idea." That voice can mean the difference between a good dive and a bad one, or in some cases, the difference between life and death.

Rescue Skills

At one time, every Open Water course contained basic rescue skills such as bringing an unconscious diver up from depth, rescue tow to shore while removing gear, and getting control of a panicked diver. These skills are now often reserved for the actual Rescue Diver course, which most divers never take. As we have seen in several cases described in an earlier chapter, lack of basic rescue skills resulted in dive buddies not knowing how to assist their buddy, and in at least three of these cases, contributed to a fatal outcome. The push to shorten classes and, by necessity, eliminate skills, has left us with untold numbers of accidents waiting to happen on every dive boat and shore diving site in the world. There have been countless incidents in which injury or death was avoided due only to dumb luck, not skill.

Pre-dive equipment checks alone are not sufficient to protect the diver in the event of an emergency requiring assistance. By keeping basic rescue skills sharp and actually instructing divers in these procedures before they even hit OW checkouts, we lessen the risk of someone dying. At a minimum, we need to practice the assist of an unconscious diver to the surface, assist of a diver who has lost his or her means of buoyancy control, supporting a diver at the surface, assisting a panicked diver, ditching weight systems, and basic tows. The agency I teach for still includes these skills in OW class, and I am free to add skills that I feel will benefit my students for the dives they will do and the locations they may choose. I will often add a no-mask swim and ascent to OW checkouts (which we have done in the pool), and every dive in my Advanced Open Water (AOW) class will include a rescue or assist of some type. Out of air (OOA) drills -- previously practiced in the pool -- may occur at any time during any activity as training progresses, because this is how OOA emergencies occur on actual dives. Proper buddy position and techniques must be practiced throughout. For my AOW class, this is a basic safety issue that if blatantly ignored or disregarded, will result in a fail for the class and no card issued.

Choosing the Right Dive Buddy

Many divers regularly dive with the same person. They know each other's skills and limitations and have established protocols for the majority of their dives. But what about those who do not dive with a regular buddy? As an instructor, I often find myself diving with new buddies. Even when not teaching, my diving interests and training often result in me diving with many different people of various skill levels, from new OW divers to experienced tech divers; these divers may have come from any number of different agencies and training programs as well. This is not an issue for me, as one of the things I have worked to achieve is the ability to dive with most anyone and be a good buddy to them. That does not always mean *they* are the best dive buddy, but being responsible for my safety and that of my teammates, I choose to develop the skills and knowledge to be up to the task. This includes familiarizing myself with the skills, training, knowledge, and attitude of my new dive buddy. We will begin with a meeting to get to know each other, perhaps do a dive or two before taking on anything challenging, and just feel each other out.

But what if you're a new diver who has not been around many other divers? How do you discover the best dive buddies and choose one who will be best for you? You can frequent local dive sites, join a dive club, and join message boards. You can ask your instructor to pair you with local divers and include you on trips; you can even ask to go along on checkout dives with other students after you have been certified. In choosing a buddy, you will need to develop a knack for recognizing the signs of a good partner and trusting your own instincts. Once a likely buddy is identified, you should dive together as much as possible in safe conditions where you can get to know each other and learn how to work well together.

Potential buddies obviously need to evaluate each other's skills and training, but also need to consider each other's interests and attitudes. Divers of equal skill and training do not necessarily make good buddies. One diver may love wrecks while the other may prefer reef dives. The skills junkie may not be a good match for the diver who is content with maintaining fair skills and just having fun. We may have heard that underwater photographers make less then desirable dive buddies, but they can be fun to dive with if we take the right attitude about the dive. Each dive with an underwater photographer is an opportunity to practice our buddy attentiveness, work on buoyancy skills, propulsion techniques, and observation skills. It can be one of diving's more rewarding experiences if we choose to make it one. When choosing a dive buddy, we have all the power in the world. There is no reason to team up with someone who gives you a feeling of unease or concern. It's better to call the dive or hire a professional for the dive. When traveling as a single diver, we seldom have the time to get to know a new diver as well as we'd like. Diving with what are affectionately known as "insta-buddies" can be fun, rewarding, and educational... or a disaster.

This means that we always, even when diving with a buddy, have to be prepared to save our own skin. We also have to be prepared to end a dive alone and get back to shore or on the boat if our new "friend" decides to deviate from the plan, disappears, or is just too scary to continue the dive with! Numerous issues can arise with these insta-buddies, including lack of communication, use of different hand signals, different goals, and different basic practices. Some divers seriously overstate their qualifications and skills, which does not become apparent until a dive has actually commenced. Unfortunately, this is a common occurrence.

Personal Responsibility

Finally, proper use of buddy skills depends on your sense of responsibility for yourself. The best dive buddy will value and practice self-sufficiency, another topic that I feel is underemphasized in many OW classes. Self-sufficiency is sometimes confused with solo diving (diving without a buddy); some divers do this, but this is not what we are talking about. Self-sufficiency, as used here, is nothing more than the ability to extricate oneself from a situation without assistance from a buddy, should it be necessary. This is nothing more than having what should be in the tool box of every certified diver from the time they receive their OW card.

The stated objective for newly certified OW divers is to be able to plan, execute, and return safely from dives in conditions equal to or better than those in which they trained, with a buddy of equal skills and training. This is a simple, clear, and seemingly definitive statement. It begs the question of why so many certified divers are uncomfortable, uneasy, unskilled, or simply unable to dive in even the most benign conditions without a dive professional present. It is troubling to me that these divers are being sent out without the basic buddy skills necessary to safely enjoy the sport, despite the existence of a clear set of standards which should prevent exactly this issue.

I hope that this section has caused you to think and to evaluate yourself, your buddy, and your training as it applies to the buddy system. It is meant to draw attention to trends that are needlessly increasing the risks of SCUBA diving.

If you are an instructor reading this, perhaps it is causing you to evaluate your methods and see how introducing some or all of these practices may aid and benefit your own students. After all, isn't the goal of every good instructor to provide students with the tools and knowledge that will aid them in their pursuit and enjoyment of the sport? The needs and interests of the student must always come before the needs of the shop, operator, or agency. If this doesn't remain our top priority we may soon see the day when injuries and deaths become more common, opening the door for things no one wants to see, like government regulation, increased insurance costs, and reduced site access. It makes far more sense to restore what were once basic skills in every OW course, thus improving the safety of our students while ensuring the survival of our sport as a whole.

I know that this section may cause some controversy, but controversy is good if it fosters discussion, thought, and a beneficial change to the status quo. We cannot prevent medical issues, the environment, and sometimes stupidity from taking the lives of divers, but we can make every effort to see that buddy separation is greatly reduced and perhaps eliminated as a cause of diver deaths.

©2010 James A Lapenta – Solo diver or missing his buddy?
Puerto Rico

NOTES

Chapter Four
Dive Planning

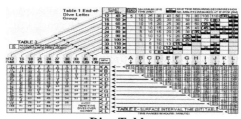

Dive Tables

Dive planning is another area that has recently received less attention in training, resulting in divers who cannot plan even the most basic of dives. This in turn has resulted in a number of injuries and some fatalities while doing what are known as "trust me" dives. Some of those were discussed in the previous section and will be looked at more closely in Chapter Six.

It is a common misconception that dive planning takes place just at the dive site, or perhaps on the way there. The fact is that it begins when the decision is made to dive at all, as was noted in the Safe Diving Practices chapter. We'll now go into more detail while looking at the mental and emotional benefits of dive planning. These factors and the very real part they play in diver safety cannot be overlooked. A properly prepared diver is far safer and a better choice as a buddy than is one who has all the latest gear, numerous certification cards, and hundreds of dives yet is uncertain, indecisive, preoccupied to the point of distraction, and goes into the water with no clear purpose.

Mental preparation for a dive is a complex process involving many factors. While more experienced divers may appear to require less preparation, this is a misconception. It is likely that

41

even more preparation is actually occurring, but due to experience and training the process has become more efficient and streamlined. More experienced divers may not need to spend as much time going over a site map because they know the area well, but their knowledge of the site increases the amount of information they will process in preparing for the dive. While the first-time diver may consider the usual depth, visibility, temperature, and current if any, the experienced diver may also take into account bottom composition, recent rains, and other environmental aspects. More experienced divers may also consider the number of other divers in the water, the time of day which could mean increased or decreased diver traffic, tides (if present), and even surface temperature. They will also plan dives with more attention to navigation and complex courses. All of these variables put added stress divers. How efficiently they can process this information can have huge effects on their mental state.

Let's look now at how new divers can make their own mental process more efficient and aid in dive planning. Why, as new divers, would we do this? The answer is the same as for all the skills that we work on -- or should -- continuously. That answer is safety. A diver who is continuously striving to improve is usually a safer diver. When we improve the mental preparation process we reduce stress, uncertainty, and indecision. We increase confidence (as opposed to bravado) and situational awareness. Such divers are more attentive to their surroundings, their buddies, and themselves. So, where do we start?

In my opinion, the first place to begin this process is in the Open Water Class. If the diver is already certified, then the next best place is this book! Thought you'd like that. But seriously, it is not far from the truth. The best place is under the guidance of an experienced diver or instructor who is a true role model of the process. These divers can be found at most every local training site. They are the ones who seem to have everything organized, their gear is well maintained, and if approached are willing to discuss what they do and how they do it without bragging or boasting.

Getting back to the Open Water Class, the most effective way I have found to foster this process is by having the students think for themselves as soon as possible. This is done by encouraging them to actively participate in the classroom and be an integral part of the planning process for each pool session. There has been a movement in dive training towards doing things strictly by the book; now there are online courses that give the student diver a prescribed amount of information with little or no opportunity for discussion with the instructor until a later time. I have found that students often have questions and want or even need answers *now*. Some of those answers may not be in the book but in the personal experiences of the instructor. Computers do not yet have "personal experiences" to fall back on and draw from. The underwater world is a dynamic and ever-changing environment which no computer can experience. The student also can't get the benefit of this experience from taking a book home, reading it, answering some questions, and then having a quick review with an instructor where time may not permit detailed and in-depth discussion. Students may not realize just how important the material is and think they understand it, when they have actually missed a critical point. Without involved, in-person instruction, such a gap in understanding might never become obvious until it has resulted in a problem after the diver has been certified.

The good educator will make sure students *do* fully understand the material. He or she will not only cover the required material, but add to it from personal experience, suggest other sources of information, and encourage students to think for themselves and ask questions. The first time a student asks a question is when the mental preparation truly begins. It is now up to the student to continue the process, and to the instructor to guide the student through the process of becoming a diver capable of independent thought. It is by developing this independence that you begin to streamline the dive planning process. Divers each have their own ways of processing information and translating it into action that works for them. The more this is practiced, the more efficient and automatic the process becomes. It becomes second nature to take certain factors into consideration. Which factors are prioritized is largely a matter of personal choice, but the instructor can help to ensure that the necessities are always covered. To do this, it is necessary to place as much emphasis on the planning skill as on other basic skills.

The instructor can foster this mindset in students by making sure they set up their gear as many times as possible, do their own weight checks for every class, keep track of their own air supplies, and when possible, choose what skills they wish to work on during free-swim times. When divers are this actively involved in the early stages of training, they begin to appreciate the thought that goes into a dive. This has the effect of shaping the mental processes involved in planning successful dives. When the mental aspects of the dive are taken into consideration, it has a profound effect on safety, and that should be the focus of every diver and instructor.

Now that the student is acting and thinking like a diver, it is important to look at the emotional effect this has. Though too seldom addressed in OW courses, it is a fact that one's emotional state can have a great effect on the success of a dive. Emotions can mean the difference between a successful, safe dive and one that ends in tragedy. When we say emotions, we are talking about those that may affect our judgment to the extent that critical items are overlooked. The emotions most likely to do this are nervousness, apprehension, and outright fear. On the other end of the spectrum, excitement and overconfidence can also have adverse effects if they take the place of common sense.

Nervousness, apprehension, and fear have the tendency to cause hesitation and may result in improper entries, delayed reactions to natural occurrences, and delayed reactions to problems encountered by other divers. While all are potential problems, the last is perhaps the most significant. Time is critical when another diver is in trouble. A delayed reaction can mean the difference, literally, between life and death. Nervousness and apprehension can actually enhance parts of the planning process while detracting from others. For example, the diver who is nervous about running out of air may spend extra time going over the actual air supply and not pay attention to the amount of weight needed to compensate for a new wet suit or one of greater or lesser thickness. Because any overlooked detail can

44

potentially contribute to an accident, overcoming these emotions is critical. That can best be done by ensuring that the diver receives the best possible training. Unfortunately, the instructor who addresses the emotional aspects of dive planning is not the norm in these times of accelerated, abbreviated training.

Many students now are lucky if they even get basic training in dive planning. New drivers are often trained to expect that they will be diving with a divemaster or instructor at all times. In some cases this may be true, and this itself may be the root cause of the anxiety. Once some divers leave the safety of the pool and classroom and get into open water, it soon becomes apparent that they really are not ready to be there. For example, their buoyancy skills are not sufficient, resulting in the fear of a rapid descent or ascent that has them constantly adjusting the BC with the inflator. Such divers may add weight to avoid a rapid ascent, but what this does is require them to add more air to the BC to offset the weight. Should they ascend just a bit too fast, Boyle's Law takes over and the increased air in the BC expands more rapidly than expected. Because the diver can't dump air fast enough and was already afraid of just such an emergency, panic may set in and result in a case of DCS or worse. If the diver should even momentarily hold his or her breath, an embolism or other lung overexpansion injury may occur.

The result of training, then, can be that instructors actually, if unwittingly, create what they should be trying to eliminate. I am convinced that this is in no way intentional; it is the result of inattention to the emotional responses of the diver. I firmly believe that every professional development course from Divemaster to Instructor should include a section dealing with the emotional responses of students to the underwater world, as well as the physical and mental responses. When the emotional aspect of dive planning is not considered, the student is denied a crucial aspect of the training necessary to become a safe and competent diver. By focusing on the emotional aspects, the diver is taught to listen to the small inner voice that may say, "This day is not a good day to dive." It may be the voice that has a diver questioning the training of a new buddy or stopping to reevaluate an entire dive plan. This is not necessarily a bad thing. In fact, it may save a diver from taking foolish risks.

Those risks could include dives for which the diver is not fully prepared, trained for, or for which there has been insufficient experience. When the diver encounters these situations and feels unease or discomfort, it is time to make a choice. That choice is entirely up to the diver. It is now based on training, experience, skills, and good judgment. That judgment is a combination of the diver's knowledge, mental state, and emotional health. Coupled with a realistic assessment of one's own abilities, an accurate and informed decision can be made. This is the very core of successful dive planning and will result in a safe and enjoyable experience for everyone concerned.

NOTES

Chapter Five
Gas Management

Gas management refers to keeping track of our air supply but also includes calculating the amount we will use on a dive, the amount we need to keep in reserve for emergencies, and selection of our cylinders. When we enter the water on SCUBA, we have a finite amount of air for our use which is carried in our SCUBA tanks. How much air we need to take with us is determined by the time and the depth of our planned dive, and the amount of air we each consume. That last factor is often referred to as our Surface Air Consumption (SAC) rate.

We may hear divers talking about their SAC rates because a critical aspect of dive planning is the amount of air required to complete the dive. You have most likely been taught to never let your tank drop below 500 psi. Perhaps you've sometimes been given a set pressure at which to turn a dive in order to return to the surface with a good safety margin. But just how much *time* do these strategies give us? You know that as we go deeper, we use more air. You learned in your Open Water class that for every atmosphere (ATA) of depth your air usage doubles, triples, quadruples, etc. You were probably given examples of this using an 80 cu ft cylinder lasting one hour at the surface. That cylinder would last 30 minutes at 2 ATA, 20 minutes at 3 ATA, 15 minutes at 4 ATA, and so on. But what if the tank lasts longer than an hour? How do we determine how much air we will use to a greater degree of accuracy? We determine our SAC rate by using a formula based on how much air we use at a given depth for a set period of time. Once we do this, we can determine to a great degree of accuracy just how much air we will use on any dive.

The first step is to determine how much air we are using. To do this, we use a dive during which we swim a course for a set period of time at a consistent depth (which also allows us to practice good buoyancy control!). Let's say that one of our dives takes place at 35 feet. We will first note the time and our starting air pressure. We will then swim for perhaps 10 minutes and record our air pressure after the swim. For the purposes of this example, we will assume we used 230 psi during our 10 minute swim at 35 feet.

Our first step in determining our SAC rate is to convert the depth (d) to atmosphere absolute (ATA) using the following formula:

$$ATA = d/33 + 1$$
$$ATA = 35/33 + 1$$
$$ATA = 1.06 + 1$$
$$ATA = 2.06$$

Our second step is to determine our rate of air usage during our test dive:

$$230 \text{ psi}/10 \text{ minutes} = 23 \text{ psi per minute}$$

Finally, we can determine our SAC rate by dividing the air consumed at depth by the actual ATA. This gives us our SAC rate in psi per minute:

$$SAC = \text{psi used}/ATA$$
$$SAC = 23/2.06$$
$$SAC = 11.17 \text{ psi per minute}$$

When using this formula for gas planning, we should round up and use 12 psi per minute to give us an added margin of safety. Now that we know what our SAC rate is, we can use that number to determine how many psi we will use for any given depth by converting that depth to ATA and multiplying it by our SAC rate. If we wish to use volume of breathing gas rather than pressure for our planning, we need a value that deals with cubic feet used per minute rather than psi used per minute. This is where Respiratory Minute Volume (RMV) comes in.

Your SAC rate is specific to the tank you are using, while your RMV is not. This is important because 2000 psi in a high pressure cylinder such as an aluminum 80 (AL80) is not the same as that in a low pressure 85. When planning the amount of gas needed for a dive for instance, the volume of gas in an AL80 at 2000 psi is approximately 53.34 cu ft. However, in a low pressure steel 85, that 2000 psi is roughly 65 cu ft. This can be very important when diving with buddies using different size tanks. In this case, knowing air consumption in volume allows the team to base the plan on actual volume of air used so that we know at a given time how much air is available to each diver. For example, let's take the SAC rate of 11.17 psi that we calculated above, and convert it to RMV. To do so, we need to determine the psi per cubic foot capacity of the cylinder we are using. To do this, we divide the rated capacity of the tank by the working pressure. For an AL80 this would be:

$$80 \text{ cu ft/ } 3000 \text{ psi} = .026 \text{ cu ft/psi}$$

We can now determine our RMV by multiplying our SAC by our baseline, which is the capacity of the tank in cu ft per psi. Remember, we rounded our SAC rate up from 11.17 psi to 12 psi for extra conservatism:

$$RMV = SAC \text{ x tank capacity}$$
$$RMV = 12 \text{ psi/minute x .026 cu ft/psi}$$
$$RMV = .31 \text{ cu ft/minute}$$

Since we used numbers obtained by swimming, this is what we call a working rate. If we were resting or swimming against a current, we could use the same formulas and determine our resting and hard-working rates and average them. You can see where being able to determine gas usage would be valuable in planning a dive requiring concentration on other factors. We still need to monitor our air supply but we can also rest assured that we have enough gas for the given dive. We need to note that for the sake of safety, the plan will be based on the SAC rate of the diver who consumes the most air.

In planning our dives, we also need to take into account the amount of air we have available. Now that we know how to determine usage in volume and psi, we can set turn pressures (the point at which we turn the dive and head back for the entry point) more accurately. We can be sure that we have enough air and also leave ourselves a good margin of safety. For example, if a team has identical AL80 tanks with 3000 psi to start the dive and we want to return with no less than 500 psi, we have an actual usable gas supply of 2500 psi available to us.

Converting this to cubic feet gives us a usable supply of 65 cu ft. If we are using RMV and we know our dive will be done at 33 ft (2 ATA) we can use a rate of .62 cu ft per minute (.31 x 2 ATA) to calculate that our tank will last us approximately 104 minutes. We determine this by dividing 65 cu ft (our available air) by our RMV at 2 ATA which is .62 cu ft per minute.

There are other methods of planning our air supply that do not require such involved calculations, such as the rule of thirds. This states that we use 1/3 of our air supply for our descent and first part of the dive, 1/3 for our return and ascent, and 1/3 held in reserve for emergencies. To be extra safe and conservative, some use the rule of thirds coupled with the 500 psi rule (which is the rule you are given by boat operators and dive shops who do not want completely empty tanks coming back). This results in a usable supply of 2500 psi in an 80 cu ft tank, so we would plan the dive in this way:

2500/3 = 833.3 psi for our descent and first part of the dive
833.3 psi for our return and ascent
833.3 psi held in reserve for emergencies

Using these numbers, we would do the dive as follows: We enter the water with 3000 psi and swim the first part of the dive. After using 833.3 psi, we are left with 2166.7 psi, which would be our cue to begin our swim back to the entry point also called our turn pressure. If we use the same amount of gas on the return leg (833.3 psi), we have 1333.4 psi left at the end of the dive. As you can see, this leaves us with a fair amount of gas should an emergency arise.

Even if we do not use the 500 psi rule and assume we have 3000 psi available to us, the rule of thirds would still leave us with 1000 psi at the end of the dive. Assuming no emergency arises, this still allows us to meet the 500 psi rule and have some air in reserve. This is the ideal. Reality is not quite as rigid and precise. Depending on conditions, the numbers here can be -- and often are -- rounded off. What usually happens is the diver will use 750-900 psi on the descent and swim out, another 750-900 psi on the swim back, and end up at the anchor line with 1200-1500 psi in reserve. On shallow reef dives (perhaps 40 foot maximum depth), this is common. Many dive operators set a time limit of one hour per dive. If divers arrive back at the line with plenty of reserve air and still have time left, it is perfectly acceptable to spend some time swimming around under the boat until one hits 750-900 psi and then begin the ascent and safety stop. The important thing is to avoid being far away from the exit point (whether boat or shore), running out of air, or exceeding No Decompression Limits (NDLs). While it's true that on open water recreational dives, the surface is always an option, there are times when heavy boat traffic makes this a poor choice. Also, it is always easier to swim underwater with SCUBA gear than on the surface. The rule of thirds can and should be modified to take into account differing cylinder sizes between buddies. If one diver is using an 80 cu ft tank and the other is using a 100 cu ft tank, the turn pressure should be governed by the smaller cylinder.

An exception to this would be if the user of the larger cylinder has a SAC rate higher than that of the person using the 80 cu ft tank. This is common when new divers are accompanied by those with more experience. As divers gain experience and become more comfortable with the underwater environment and their equipment, their air consumption tends to improve. A relaxed diver is one who moves more efficiently, swims at a steadier pace, and therefore consumes less air. Some believe that female divers tend to use less air than their male counterparts. I know of no scientific evidence to support this but have observed it many times. I cannot discount it and have sometimes recommended to couples just starting out that they consider asking for a larger tank for the male diver. This is, of course, after having assessed them and determining that this is a workable solution in their case. What this does is allow the rule of thirds to be observed, yet still allow for a longer dive. When using this modification, it important to determine the SAC rates of the divers and take into account actual tank volumes to ensure that the proper emergency reserve is still maintained. While this rule usually works very well for the average recreational dive and the reserve is adequate, there are times when it is prudent to be even more specific as to what an acceptable reserve is. In this case we are able to use another method of gas reserve planning known as Rock Bottom.

Rock Bottom is used by many divers and is especially useful when planning dives that may involve more effort, be done in less than optimal conditions, or require the divers to expend more effort on an ascent. Deep dives, low visibility dives, or those done in cold water are some examples of these conditions. Basically, Rock Bottom is the minimum reserve pressure divers should have in their tanks to execute a safe ascent -- with a safety stop -- in the event of an emergency while sharing air. As this is considered an emergency ascent, it is done using the "working SAC rate" to give the greatest level of conservatism, and takes into account the cylinder sizes of the team or buddy pair. The calculations for this are quite involved and frankly, beyond the scope of this work. More detailed information on Rock Bottom is readily available for those who are curious to know about it, and can easily be found in an Internet search.

Now that we have covered some basic gas management methods, the question is why do we need them? You might be thinking, "Can't I just follow the divemaster or guide and let him worry about my air supply?" Sadly, the answer is that you can, but are you really okay with allowing a stranger to have that much control over your safety? I am not. As a trained Open Water diver, you should not need or want to delegate that responsibility to anyone other than yourself. It is unfair to ask that of anyone else. An exception is if you specifically hire a divemaster for that purpose, but even then there is always the possibility that something could happen to him or her, leaving you on your own. There is also the chance that your divemaster may estimate your air usage on some average made up of other divers he or she has guided. This if fine if that average is on the high side of your actual numbers, but not so good if it is on the other end of the scale. That 80 cu ft tank that lasted other divers over an hour on a dive to a maximum depth of 70 feet with sufficient reserves may not work for you. If you tend to use more air than the "average" diver, you could find yourself in serious trouble.

This all relates back to the ideas of personal responsibility, safe diving practices, and good dive planning. I do not agree with the idea of allowing someone else to decide what ultimately may be my fate if things go south, or to put my life in the hands of a stranger who does not know me. Some dive operations have a reputation for pushing the limits beyond what would be considered safe diving. They routinely take divers whose recommended limit is no deeper than 60 feet on dives beyond that, sometimes to depths approaching the recommended limits for highly experienced recreational divers.

The recommended limit for recreational divers does vary according to agency. Scuba Educators International, the agency I certify divers through, recommends a limit of 100 feet for recreational divers. Our tables do go to 130 feet and even include decompression tables, but the times beyond 100 feet are so short with a nice slow descent rate that there is really not much time for sightseeing. It is only if the diver has a specific purpose or task that they should be going to those depths. With other agencies, the maximum recommended depth (with a deep specialty certification) is 130 feet.

Despite these standards, it is a common practice for some operations to take divers to those depths without knowing the divers or their air usage. The most common phrase used to justify the safety of these dives is, "We do it all the time!" That is not good enough for me or for my students. This brings us to our next topic: dealing with these "trust me" dives.

NOTES

Chapter Six
"Trust Me" Dives

This chapter deals with those dives that often replace common sense and good training. Such dives occur when divers choose to blindly follow a divemaster (DM), dive guide, or even instructor without taking the time to plan their own dives. This is apparently due to a number of factors, including the lack of education in dive planning in the Open Water class, students who are comfortable with not taking responsibility for themselves, and the reinforcement of these ideas by instructors. The last is one of the most disturbing issues, as students are given the impression or even told that they don't need to take responsibility for themselves. Students are given the false impression that the DM or guide on the boat will not only plan their dives but keep them safe. This was discussed in the section on diver responsibility, but it is so important that it really deserves a separate chapter of its own. We have looked at the importance of dive planning and gas management; these are core skills that even new Open Water divers should have, and should never be neglected through blind reliance on others.

What leads to a diver agreeing to a "trust me" dive varies with the diver, the geographic location of the dives, and the initial training the diver received. Other factors can be the diver's buddy or teammates, divers who may not be buddies but are still part of the group, and even financial considerations. We'll look at each of these factors in more detail now.

When a diver receives bare-minimum training, a number of things are affected. Deficits can be seen in physical skills, knowledge base, and judgment. Shortened training necessitates leaving out some information. Items such as gas planning are often not covered in great detail even though this is a crucial factor in dive planning. This lack of knowledge is readily apparent when it comes time to go out and dive on one's own, and is what leaves the diver at the mercy of the guide or dive operator when it comes time to plan and execute a dive.

Not knowing much more than the "Be back with 500 psi," rule, divers have to trust the judgment of strangers to say whether or not the dives they will be doing are safe. This is not the way one conducts safe SCUBA dives. Why do we trust people we don't know to determine what is a safe dive for us? They most likely have never seen us dive before, do not know our skill level other than perhaps by what card we have, have no idea what our air consumption is, and do not know our actual comfort level in the water. The question then is how can they make an informed and accurate judgment? *Well, quite simply they can't!* They can only look at previous divers of somewhat equal skill and training and hope for the best. This is not a good way to conduct a dive, yet it is being done all the time. Divers, perhaps without knowing it, are at the mercy of the dive operator. The unfortunate part is that many divers find this totally acceptable. Going back to the idea of personal responsibility, how can divers feel comfortable with this? They are comfortable with it because they don't know any better. They have no idea just how risky these dives can be and sadly, these divers are often personally responsible for this lack of knowledge.

This may sound harsh, but it's true. Divers elect to get certified, having seen the ads for warm locations, fun, and quick certifications. Time is not taken to research the different agencies and training methods. As in other areas, the idea of instant gratification overshadows common sense. People will spend more time researching a new flat screen television than an activity in which they could possibly lose their life. Think about that for a minute. Does it make sense that this is the case? Not to me. Those who are looking for a course that is fast, easy, and has just enough to get by will be disappointed if they seek instruction from me. The class I offer takes 6-8 weeks and averages around 40 hours of classroom, pool, and open water training.

Proper training prepares divers to take care of themselves so that they will never be tempted to take part in "trust me" dives. Students are the ones who make many of the decisions during training. While there are certain standards that must be met, there are opportunities for students to make decisions on what skills they wish to work on, evaluate how much weight they will use, consider how much time they have based on the amount of air they use, and when conditions may require different equipment such as a thicker exposure suit. When my students get to open water I make a real effort to let them lead the dives whenever possible, use their newfound skills in actual real life situations, and make them responsible for much of the dive planning. "Trust me" dives are discussed in detail with heavy emphasis on why they are not a good idea. When you elect to go on a trip and spend a great deal of money, time, and effort to make sure the trip is a success, why would you then abdicate responsibility for your life?

This is what doing a "trust me" dive really is. The diver turns over his or her life to a stranger with less thought than would be dedicated to deciding what to have for lunch. These divers have been taught and encouraged to just follow the DM or guide, rather than spend more time developing skills and values like extensive dive planning, self-sufficiency, and personal responsibility. The result is divers who need their hands held throughout the entire process of the dive. From getting on the boat, setting up the equipment, deciding where to go, and entering the water, to in some cases, even getting back on the boat, the diver is under the impression that he or she is under the protection and care of the "professional." Such divers don't have to think for themselves about what they are doing. Like sheep, they blindly follow the shepherd, even when they are led into places they really should not be.

We looked at one such incident in the section on responsibility. New divers followed a guide on a dive that was not only beyond their recommended depth but also consisted of poor buddy procedures, divers of vastly different experience, and at least one who had not been in the water in over a year. In addition, there was no hard bottom for that dive shallower than the 342 ft depth the deceased diver reached before his rapid ascent. This is a case where a "trust me" dive resulted in a dead diver. It did not have to happen. All it would have taken was one of the other divers speaking up forcefully enough to insist on a change of site to one with a hard bottom at 60 feet, the recommended maximum depth for an open water diver. But all had been conditioned to trust the judgment of the "professional" and as a result, a diver is no longer with us. Just as an aside, the diver's fiancée was on the dive as well; they were to have been married in a couple of weeks.

A common place for "trust me" dives to occur is Cozumel, Mexico. Divers with Open Water certifications are routinely taken to a feature called the "Devil's Throat." It is a swim-through that begins at approximately 80 feet and empties out at around 130 feet, over a vertical wall that drops into the abyss. This dive is actually a cavern dive with an overhead and sections where two divers cannot pass in proper buddy position. So why are divers being taken into this cavern on 80 cu ft tanks? Why are they allowed to actually approach the very limits of a recreational dive without having to plan the dive based on their own SAC rates? What happens if something goes wrong? Who is there to rescue you if you are the last diver and the DM and your buddy are far ahead, perhaps even out of sight? No one. So why would you think it is okay to allow a stranger to plan this dive for you? I don't see this as a recreational dive for Open Water divers or even for those with an Advanced Open Water diver card when that card is the result of little more than a tour of what can be called advanced dives.

"Trust me" dives are not just those led by a DM. They can be led by another certified diver who is not a professional but may have more experience. However, more experience does not always mean more common sense. Divers often get into trouble on "trust me" dives with buddies who have gotten away with doing risky dives more by dumb luck than real skill. These dives are extremely risky for newer divers. Again, the new diver may have been conditioned to trust the more "experienced" diver and believe that it will be okay as long as the leader makes the decisions. There are many cases throughout history where blindly following the "leader" has resulted in terrible consequences. What has to be taken into consideration is that in many cases *the leader may have been trained by the same person who neglected to instill a real sense of responsibility in the new diver.* This is another important point to ponder when deciding if doing a certain dive is a good idea.

Peer pressure often results in "trust me" dives. A new OW diver is diving with a group of divers who may hold advanced cards. Rather than leave the OW diver out, they convince their new friend to do a deep dive or night dive. They insist they will keep the new diver safe; the diver knows this is not a good idea, but being conditioned to trust a more experienced diver, relents and goes on the dive. Maybe everything goes okay and no one gets hurt. Or maybe the divers get separated and one panics and does a rapid ascent. An injury may occur because a diver trusted someone else rather than relying on training and good judgment. It does not have to happen. In fact, it never has to happen and it is very easy to prevent -- in theory. In theory, all that needs to occur is for agencies, shops, instructors, and resorts to insist that all divers be responsible for themselves.

If this were to happen, "trust me" dives would soon be replaced by divers planning their own dives and diving those plans. In my opinion, it would also have the effect of requiring divers to be trained to higher standards.

A thread on a diving message board I frequent was about two divers who were "led" on a dive beyond their comfort level, or so it appeared based on their version of events. What actually came out was that the DM gave a briefing where he detailed what he was going to do, what the site offered, the depth *he* would be at, and that the divers were free to follow him or dive their own plans. It was also recommended that they develop their own plans and stick to them. As certified divers, they should be able to do this. The couple chose to abort the dive based on their comfort level but then turned around and blamed the DM for taking them on a bad dive in what they considered to be poor conditions. This was an example of a "do not trust me" dive. To me, this is how all dives should be conducted. The divers were given the option to plan their own dive and if that plan was the same or similar to the DM's, fine. If not, they were free to develop another one and stick to that. This is the kind of operation I want to dive with! One that does not insult my intelligence but rather, allows and even requires that I do what my training tells me I should do. What a novel approach to recreational diving this is! One that is welcome and long overdue.

NOTES

Chapter Seven
When to Get More Training and Why

Beyond your Open Water class and basic recreational diving is a world of opportunities. Some of these opportunities require additional training if you want to pursue them safely, but when and how should you get this training?

It is unwise to take on advanced training before you have had time to practice basic skills and get comfortable with them. There are agencies and shops that encourage divers into taking more training right after Open Water. I feel this is a mistake if the student will be introduced to new skills, because all diving skills are built upon the basics. Open Water skills need to be practiced to some degree before they can become the solid foundation upon which the student can effectively add advanced training. I believe any diver should be able to perform all basic skills midwater and in good trim, and this becomes even more important if the diver takes on new skills. Whether it be Advanced Open Water, Underwater Navigation, or even Rescue, the ability to remove/replace a mask, recover a regulator, and use non-silting kicks is necessary for successful completion of these classes. Full achievement of these skills may mean extra time with an instructor for some students. Diver safety is the most important priority, so whatever is necessary to achieve that is what must be done -- look for an instructor who is willing to adapt the training schedule to your needs. If my students need more dives, I invite them to join me when I go diving locally, which makes for a more relaxed and enjoyable time. There is no charge, but I will pass on pointers and if asked, critique their technique. I do this because it makes it easier for them and for me to be sure they have the basics down before giving them new skills. My AOW class involves many new skills and it is possible to fail the class, so I want to be sure that they are prepared before they begin. I do not sell certifications -- I provide training. Certification is earned.

Instructors should take the time to assess the skills of divers before accepting them for advanced training of any kind. There are risks involved with a number of continuing education classes that could put a less-than-comfortable diver under enough stress to cause a panic situation. Divers have a responsibility to be honest with instructors as to their reasons for wanting the training. Divers do not always realize what it is they are getting themselves into when they choose advanced training and unfortunately, a number of instructors do not point out all the risks to them. The risks during training are minimized somewhat by the presence of the instructor and his or her assistants, but there are still accidents. As I am writing this, there is a search going on for a diver who did not surface during a training dive. The real danger though, is after the class. It is imperative that divers understand the advanced card gives them access to sites and dives where the risks are much greater and things can go wrong more quickly, but *advanced training does not make them advanced divers*. Only experience will do that. If you understand this, have solid basic skills and feel ready to take on new challenges, then by all means it is time to seek out an instructor who can provide the appropriate training.

So, what training should you seek? Simply the training that will give you the skills you need. This often means the Advanced Open Water class, but is this always the best choice? The agencies, shops, and many instructors would have you think so. I, however, believe that it is not always the best choice. There are students who do not want to dive deep, at night, do search and recovery, or any number of other options available for the AOW rating. Does this mean that these divers should either be denied training or talked into the AOW card anyway? Absolutely not. The smart instructor will find or even create training that works for each student. Training that is customized to your interests will keep you more involved in the sport while still adding to your skills in a manner that improves your safety and competence in any diving you choose to do.

One area I consider essential to diver development and safety is Underwater Navigation; it is a core skill of the competent and self-sufficient diver. For those divers with good buoyancy skills who do not desire the deep, dark, or silty, this type of training offers an ideal way to advance skills while staying in the conditions they prefer. A good Navigation class will increase buddy, communication, and buoyancy skills while increasing your confidence, comfort and safety. A bad class will not only fail to provide these benefits, but may convince you that you will never get any better or are just not good enough. Advanced training should always result in you being more skilled and knowledgeable than when you started the training. For this reason, a by-the-book approach is seldom as effective as one that is tailored to individual students. Not everyone learns at the same pace or in the same manner. If you choose to take on more training, choose your instructor carefully. Some offer individualized training and some do not; some may not know how, or may believe their agency does not permit them to alter training content.

A good reason to get more training is to increase your knowledge of the underwater world and awareness of its effects on the body. Many Open Water classes have been shortened and watered down to the point that much of what used to be considered essential information is now omitted. Taking on advanced training that imparts this missing knowledge is well worth the time, effort, and expense. The information divers should be seeking includes a better understanding of physiology and the effects of diving, basic rescue skills, proper weighting with buoyancy and trim training, and a deeper understanding of the risks that SCUBA diving poses. Many divers have been led to believe that this sport is not as dangerous as it really is, that it is all fun and sun. They have also been led to believe that they will be taken care of by others. This belief can kill you.

Realizing that you are responsible for yourself and for learning the necessary skills is crucial to both safety and enjoyment. So how do you find someone to help you continue your education? That's what we'll look at next.

Notes

Chapter Eight
Choosing an Instructor
They Work for You!

Many people choose an instructor with less thought than they give to choosing a new television. My question is, why? A television does not hold your life in its hands, but the instructor you choose will. Some do not even have a choice of who the instructor will be; they sign up with a large shop and the shop assigns the students to whoever has the next class. No pre-class interview, no quick personality check to see if they mesh well, and no opportunity for the instructor to assess the fitness and interests of the student. I cannot fathom why anyone would accept this. When choosing an instructor, you need to understand that what you are doing is hiring an employee. *You* are the employer -- not the shop, not the agency, not the dive resort. You are employing this person to teach you to survive in an environment that is hostile to human life. Why would you not put serious thought into this? Why would you not interview this person and ask questions of him or her?

1. *Every agency has good instructors, great instructors, and some that are neither. So how do you find the best ones?* Here are a few things to consider: First of all, how did you hear of them? Was it an ad in the phonebook, online, or from a friend? These are all good ways of finding an instructor, but you don't usually get a lot of information to work with. Can you find online reviews of the shop or its personnel? Are you able to talk to former students and get their impressions? An instructor who has nothing to hide or fear has no problem contacting former students and getting their permission to use them as references. If you go through a shop and they assign the instructor,

can you interview them before paying any course fee? If not, why not? If you can and they do not seem like a good fit, can you change instructors? All of these should factor into your decision. Once you have satisfied yourself with these questions, what should you ask of the instructor? Bearing on my own experience as a student and now as an instructor, I can give you a list of questions. You may have others you wish to ask or there may be some on the list you may not wish to use. All of that is fine as long as you end up with an instructor who is a good fit, knows what he or she is doing, puts your interests first, and will give you the skills and knowledge necessary to dive safely and independently. So, here are some questions to ask, and why:

2. *"When did you become an instructor?"* New instructors are not necessarily bad news. They may be up on the latest trends in teaching and have recent knowledge of new theories and science. An instructor who has been teaching a long time may be set in his or her ways and teaching out of routine, but also brings many years of experience to the table.

3. *"Have you had any large gaps in your teaching career? How recently? How many courses have you taught in the past year?"* You want someone who has been teaching consistently enough to maintain sharp instructional skills. This requires teaching at least a few courses per year.

4. *"What is your certifying agency?"* While most agencies are recognized around the world, some are better known, and not just because of size. Agencies vary in the comprehensiveness of their Open Water curricula; some now leave out what many consider to be essential skills and information, while some have a reputation for producing skilled divers who need little or no supervision. Given that a SCUBA certification is a serious issue, it is in your best interest to do some personal research, deciding for yourself which agency

offers course content that best meets your needs and expectations.

5. *"How much time is required for the course?"* A comprehensive course cannot and should not be taught in two weekends, in my opinion. The course should allow you enough time to absorb the information and practice the new skills that you are given. I recommend a minimum of 40 hours between pool, classroom, and open water checkouts.

6. *"How large are the classes?"* This is important because the more students in a class, the less individual attention. Even if the instructor has certified assistants, he or she is still responsible for your instruction. In addition, a large class often leaves less time for students to just swim around and get comfortable with new skills. With no assistants, I prefer to have no more than four students in the water at a time. Remember that the size of the pool will also affect the number of students that can comfortably be accommodated at one time.

7. *"What equipment do you provide and what do I as the student need to supply?"* Some courses supply all gear while others require the students to supply things like mask, snorkel, fins and boots. If you must buy some personal gear, look for a shop that allows you to try out those items in the pool before purchase. There is no reason to spend money on gear that you soon find out does not fit or is not quite right for your style of diving.

8. *"Is your class schedule set or flexible?"* In some cases the schedule is set by the shop. This may work for some people, but I have found that many students require more flexibility due to work, school, kids, or all of the above. Many independent instructors can tailor classes around the student's schedule at little or no extra cost.

9. *"Do you teach skin diving skills?"* One of the simplest ways to build comfort in the water is to teach students basic swimming and skin diving skills. In fact, a good instructor will use the swimming and skin diving portion of the class to gauge the comfort level of their students in the water.

10. *"What methods do you use to teach proper weighting?"* Weight checks should be done at the beginning of every pool session, as described earlier in this book in the Buoyancy Control and Trim section of Chapter Two. Some students may require extra weight in the initial sessions, but by the end of pool training, they should be properly weighted and doing their own weight checks.

11. *"What methods do you use to address the panic cycle?"* Panic can kill a diver. It is brought on by stress, and stress is created by a diver being uncomfortable with a given situation. This feeling can be minimized by addressing its causes in confined water and in the classroom. The various stress triggers can be identified, as well as ways of dealing with them. This is called breaking or interrupting the panic cycle. Not every course offers this critical piece of education, so check specifically for it when you interview an instructor.

12. *"Do you teach students to perform skills in a horizontal position from the beginning of the class?"* This is another important point to clarify since divers do not dive in a vertical position. There is a small but growing trend to get divers out of the "praying-I-survive-this" position, as I call it. My own OW class and classes I assisted with before adopting horizontal training methods, invariably had students trying to kneel in the water with SCUBA gear on. Students, already nervous, would sometimes flail about trying to stay upright; some got upset enough to come close to bolting for the

surface. I have found that if students on SCUBA are taught to descend horizontally from the beginning, this stress trigger is greatly reduced or even eliminated. Basic skills are easier in a horizontal position anyway, and the position eliminates the stress of feeling unbalanced and trying not to fall over backwards.

13. *"Will I have time to just swim and practice the skills we learn?"* Some instructors will go through the skills, have the students do them, and then move quickly on to something else. This does not allow the brain sufficient time to process new information, and denies students the additional practice that would help them become fully comfortable and confident with what they are doing. Practice time is essential.

14. *"Can I sit in on a class or pool session?"* If the instructor has a class going on, they should have no problem with you observing a session.

15. *"What methods do you use to teach buoyancy and trim?"* As outlined in the chapter on basic skills there are ways to teach buoyancy using the BC, proper weighting, and using lung volume. All of these should be included in the basic class.

16. *"How much time will I get to practice these skills?"* I schedule a minimum of 20 minutes in each pool session for students to practice skills while working on buoyancy and trim. By the time students get to open water checkouts they have a good handle on how lung volume, use of the inflator and other factors such as equipment affect how buoyancy and trim work.

17. *"Do you dive with students after class has ended?"* The good instructor has no qualms about diving with students he or she has trained, without additional charge to the students. I want my students to come on

dives with me and others. They set an example of divers who are actively diving and enjoying it.

18. *"Where do you do your checkout dives?"* Most instructors and shops have certain sites they use for checkouts. Some are free, others are not. You need to ask if you will be responsible for any entry or boat fees.

19. *"How many places have you been diving?"* Why ask this? Simply because divers – including instructors – are more likely to be better divers if they have a broad range of experience and are well-versed in local diving. You would not want an instructor who has never been in cold water to teach you to dive in Minnesota in a dry suit! If you are going to dive in the Caribbean, you would want someone who has experienced saltwater to teach you, rather than someone who has never been out of the lake or quarry.

20. *"When was the last time you were diving?"* I try to get into the water at least once a month, year round. It does not always work that way, but like any other diver, an instructor needs to practice skills.

21. *"How often do you dive for fun?"* It is widely reported and acknowledged among dive instructors that those who never dive just for fun are more susceptible to burnout. Many instructors actually stop teaching after about two years because of this, and I was nearly one of them. At one time, I did nothing but training dives for several months, with no time to relax and just have fun. It became less and less enjoyable, so much so that I took a break for a while and seriously considered giving up teaching. I stopped assisting with classes and just dove for fun. I took some classes of my own to expand my knowledge and skills in technical diving disciplines. I was recharged and realized that I do enjoy teaching and passing on my love of diving to others. I learned the hard way that it has to be tempered with time for myself as well, and many other

instructors have learned the same lesson. Make sure yours is one of them.

22. *"Do you have references – former students that I can talk to?"* No quality instructor will object to this request. Get a number of names and talk to more than one if you can.

You might also ask more in-depth questions about what courses are offered, how they are taught, whether classroom is involved, and how much self-study is involved in learning the theory behind the dives and why they are done. Students who are paying for education should receive an education -- from an instructor. Self-study should *reinforce* the training, not replace it.

As you ask these questions, pay attention to the answers you get and more importantly, how you get them. None of these questions is out of line. The instructor should be more than willing to answer all of them patiently and completely, and should support your comparing his or her course with others in the area. I have in my library the standards for six different agencies – any student or potential student is welcome to see them at any time and compare them with the instruction they are receiving from me.

Remember that what you are doing is hiring an employee, an employee that is working for you. If your children are to receive instruction (with you, or in their own separate class), there should be some additional questions. Not everyone is good with kids. Kids can have special challenges – shorter attention spans, less tolerance to cold, they may tire more easily -- and these all need to be considered. I actually plan on extra class and pool time when teaching kids, just to address these issues. I have also taken an additional step for the peace of mind of the parents of my younger students: I have obtained state clearances for working with children, the same clearances required of teachers and other professionals who work with kids. I also have clearance from the Girl Scouts of the USA to teach programs for them. I have found that these clearances are a bonus to me and my classes; I encourage you to seek out instructors who make this same level of effort, even if they aren't legally required to do so. In short, when choosing an instructor or class, put the same effort into it that you would if you were hiring an employee.

While instructors do work for you, never lose sight of why you hired them. If you were able to teach yourself, you would have. The fact is that you need the knowledge, skills, experience, and expertise that only an instructor can provide. Instructors determine the tone, content and schedule of instruction, but should be doing so with your best interests in mind and with respect for your comfort level. Any time you are asked to do a skill or perform an exercise, there should be a good reason for it and a clear explanation of its importance. Instructors have an obligation to uphold the standards of their agency and shop (if they work for one), but you do not have to perform any skill you choose not to. However, if you decline a required skill, they do not have to issue a certification or even continue training. It is a partnership where you must work together, but in this one, you sign the paychecks.

Notes

Chapter Nine
What Type of Training is Best for You?

Now that you have found an instructor, you need to determine whether the training offered is the best for you. If you are seeking an Open Water course, you may have heard some say that all Open Water courses are basically the same. The fact is that they are not; there are major differences between various programs. My recommendation is to find a course that will give you all the skills to safely plan, execute, and return from a dive with a buddy of equal skill and training, and without the accompaniment of a dive professional. You should be able to do this in conditions equal to or better than those in which you were trained. Such a course should give you the skills to assist another diver should something go wrong, and help you develop your sense of responsibility to yourself and your buddy. Finally, it should give you the confidence and judgment to know when a dive is beyond your skill, training, and experience and to call the dive should those conditions arise.

The Open Water Course

The course should contain all the elements needed to fulfill these requirements. The instructor should begin by making sure you are comfortable in the water and most importantly, that you can swim. This sounds obvious, but there are some agencies that allow divers to complete swim requirements wearing mask, snorkel, and fins. This is not swimming. Some say divers don't need to know how to swim well because they will have all that gear on. I personally believe that swimming is a life skill that all people should possess, but at the very least, anyone who is going to be in or near water should know how to swim.

I believe that parents who do not teach their children to swim are guilty of neglect if they allow their children near bodies of water. If they let their kids *in* the water without knowing how to swim, those parents are guilty of abuse! I have seen a child who did not know how to swim pulled from the deep end of a pool. The parents were nowhere around. In this day and age with all the public access to swimming and swim lessons, not teaching a child to swim is inexcusable. Students should know how to swim, period. If they do not, then training should not begin until they've gotten the necessary lessons.

Next is skin diving and snorkeling skills – your course should include instruction in both of these. It should cover kicks, mask clearing, snorkel clearing, and two types of skin dives (head-first and feet-first). It should include practice time for all of these techniques. During this time, you should also be introduced to and instructed in the use of proper buddy procedures. This is done by pairing students up and insisting they remain together during every exercise; this reinforces the idea that when one is diving with a buddy in any circumstance, the partners need to stay together. The classroom material at this stage should introduce you to basic diving history, the equipment used in snorkeling and skin diving, and a discussion about basic physics and physiology. All of this material should be covered before you are ever introduced to SCUBA equipment.

The next session in the pool is when students are introduced to SCUBA gear. The instructor should start by first determining how much weight students need in whatever exposure suits they are wearing. Once proper weighting (not overweighting) is established, students should be introduced to breathing through the regulator on the surface. From this point on, each new skill is built upon those that came before. Pool sessions should focus on diver safety and comfort. This is done by taking basic skills and reinforcing them through practice and by adding to them. Gradually increased task loading builds comfort and confidence while also adding to the safety of the diver and of their buddy.

74

The classroom is where dive theory is passed on and explained; in my opinion, this necessitates face-to-face discussion. Having a student take a book home, read it, and answer a few questions only to spend a few minutes reviewing those answers with an instructor is not education. It is memorization of and parroting what was in the book. The student may or may not understand all the information. It's great if this works for you, but even *you* may not be able to tell if it has worked for you, because you can't know what you don't know. If a detail was missed in study that also never comes up in subsequent discussion, that missing knowledge could be dangerous to you at some later point. When I have students in front of me and am able to see their faces, I get immediate feedback. I know if they are getting the material, because I see the lights come on. Alternatively, I can see when those lights dim and I know that we need to slow down, stop, or review the material. Self-study material should reinforce the material taught and prepare students for the next session. It should not replace actual lectures and face-to-face discussions.

Students often do not meet the instructor until the actual start of the course, and some courses may have more than one instructor teaching different portions of the material. If the instructors are not effectively communicating with each other for any reason, content can be duplicated or even omitted. This is even more of an issue when it comes to pool training, especially during the first few sessions. Every instructor has a personal style and methods for teaching the exact same skill. To start off one way and then have to switch to a different way is not an issue for students who are completely comfortable in the water and with the skill. For the student who has any kind of issue with basic skills, however, this could prove to be a serious problem. My own experience tells me that the same approach to a skill that is successful for five people may not work with the sixth one. I have often found it necessary to modify the approach and even spend one-on-one time with a student in a private. In my classes, the skill where we most often run into this issue is mask remove/replace.

Some OW instructors are satisfied when a student is able to successfully perform this skill one time in the pool. My own instructor told me that if he demonstrated the skill and I repeated it successfully such that it was as if he was looking in a mirror, I was done with it. I thought that was how it was supposed to be. I realized the problem with this one day in open water when my mask got kicked and I had nowhere to kneel so that I could get vertical to clear it. It was an extremely uncomfortable situation, and it should not have been. It was not until later in my diving career when I went to another agency that I found out this method of teaching skills is not the norm. Not all new open water students are expected to perform the skill once and move on to something else. When I switched agencies, I discovered that some classes have students repeat skills over and over every session. Then, they add other tasks to be performed while doing the basic skill; this has the effect of getting a student comfortable with the skill in a number of different situations. In my class, students clear and remove/replace the mask at least 20 times before we get to open water. Other skills are practiced in similar fashion. By the time students get to open water, they should be able to perform all basic skills at any time during the checkout dives. They should be able to do this while swimming, hovering, and not breaking trim.

This is the kind of training that makes SCUBA diving a much more enjoyable venture for everyone. When looking for a training course, you should look for courses that offer plenty of time both to learn skills and to practice them in the pool. A course designed to get you through in four to six hours of pool time leaves you little opportunity to just swim around and practice those new skills. This is especially true if there are more than a couple people in the class, because each skill takes time for each person to perform. The presence of certified assistants doesn't necessarily help with this, because some agencies require that they can only help after the instructor has taught the skill.

When selecting an initial certification class, ask yourself what you plan to get out of it. Do you want to be able to dive with confidence and skill? Do you want to be able to plan a dive, dive that plan, and safely return from that dive on your own? Do you want to be able to go anywhere within the limits of your training and experience and not have to rely on someone else to keep you safe? If not, are you okay with hiring a private guide or divemaster to watch over you? Remember, this is the only way you can ensure that they will be looking after you, and you alone. Can you also accept the idea that if something happens to your guide, you may have to look after yourself and perhaps even rescue the guide? This is a very real possibility. Finally, are you comfortable with the fact that you are literally putting your life in the hands of a stranger? If you want to be responsible for yourself and perhaps your loved ones, determine how, when, where you will dive, and be assured in the knowledge that you can handle most any issue that comes up, then I strongly suggest that you look into a comprehensive course that will contain all the information and skills necessary to do those things. You may need to do some research to find such a course, but they do exist and are readily available to those who wish to be safe, confident, skilled, and self-sufficient divers.

Beyond the Open Water Course

The theme of skills, education, and competency should be carried over into all areas of diver training. Once you are past the Open Water certification phase, you may be encouraged to move immediately into some type of advanced training. Whether it be an Advanced Open Water (AOW) course or other specialty training course, my advice is, *don't do it!* Take some time to work on the skills that you were just presented with in the Open Water class. My own rule is to not allow a student to take any additional formal training until they have accumulated at least ten dives beyond those required in their OW course. Each student is evaluated on an individual basis, and I offer non-certification training in various areas to be sure students are ready for any advanced training they may wish to take. Some agencies require students to take the AOW class before doing anything else. This can be a problem for students who are not interested in deep diving, night diving, or some of the other areas covered by the standard AOW class. Forcing divers to take AOW training first may prevent them from ever pursuing *any* further training (which would have made them better, safer divers). We'll look at that shortly, but I'd like first to talk about the AOW class as it has traditionally been taught.

For many years, the AOW class has been offered under some systems as a "taste" of what could be considered advanced dives. I prefer to give divers the skills and knowledge to capably *handle* more advanced dives, which is why I wrote my own AOW class.

The reason for this is that the AOW certification card allows the diver to gain access to dives beyond the recommended Open Water certification limits. These might involve greater depths, night dives, dives in current, or any number of challenges the diver has not faced before. Such dives require the diver to have knowledge and skills that are beyond the scope of most Open Water courses. Even a comprehensive OW course may not give divers every skill they need to do these dives successfully and safely. This is not due to instructor neglect but reflects the simple reality of not being able to include every possible skill in an OW course. When I developed my AOW class, I chose dives and skills that would allow divers with a solid foundation in basic skills to continue their education in a meaningful way. I therefore chose the following dives to prepare divers for what are often looked at as "advanced dives" – Advanced Skills, Underwater Navigation, Night/Low Visibility, Deep, Search and Recovery, and Buddy Skills and Assist. These dives were chosen based on what I have seen divers actually wishing to do with the advanced certification, and include the "advanced" skills described on the following pages.

1. Advanced Skills -- This dive is used to enhance the OW diver's skills by reinforcing and improving basic skills as well as introducing the following new ones:
    a) Anti-silting kicking techniques consisting of frog and/or modified frog kicks, helicopter turns, and back kicks.

b) Performing basic skills while swimming and hovering, including mask remove/replace, regulator retrieval, weight remove/replace, and sharing air.

c) Shooting a lift bag to assist in ascents.

d) Reinforcing proper weighting and trim.

e) Deployment of a redundant air source (pony bottle).

2. Underwater Navigation -- This dive is used as a follow-up to the basic compass skills as performed during the OW checkouts. The basic square and triangle patterns will again be used, but the instructor will now also have the student select an object on the bottom to use as a reference at each turn. This small exercise in combined compass and natural navigation is used to illustrate the increased accuracy of this method while potentially interesting the student in further navigation training. The following skills should be emphasized and evaluated:

a) Holding the compass properly.

b) Maintaining horizontal trim, especially when making turns.

c) Maintaining position in the water column at a steady pace.

d) Buddy awareness and communication.

e) Accuracy.

f) Attention to detail and selection of landmarks.

g) Measuring distance through kicks, time, air consumption, or a line.

3. Night/Low Visibility -- This dive is used to familiarize the student with the fascinating world of diving without natural light. The use of dive lights, strobes, markers, and new methods of communicating with the dive buddy are introduced. Skills include:

a) Buoyancy control.

b) Light use and selection.

c) Use of strobe or marker to mark the anchor or down line.

d) Buddy contact and communication.

e) Lost diver procedures.

f) Navigation.

g) Site choice.

4. Deep Dive -- The deep dive is one of the primary reasons that divers take the AOW course; they wish to do dives exceeding the recommended OW limit of 60 feet. Whether it is a wreck, wall, or reef, there is usually some reason for them to get a card that will demonstrate to a resort or boat operation that they are qualified to do the dive. Unfortunately, this is usually the dive that also presents the most risk to the diver. Increased air usage demands a better understanding of management of the air supply. When doing these dives, it is necessary to watch time and depth with much greater attention; the No Decompression Limits are reached much more quickly. You may start looking at redundant air sources such as pony bottles. It is essential to be sure you get the proper equipment and know how to use it. Obviously, the effects of nitrogen narcosis need to be covered. Skills on this dive include:

a) Buoyancy control.

b) Horizontal descent and ascent.

c) Maintaining rate of descent.

d) Situational awareness via tests to judge effects of narcosis.

e) Alternate Air Share ascent to staged tanks

f) Communication.

g) Management of air supply.

h) Deployment of stage/pony bottle.

i) Final ascent utilizing deep stops.

5. Search and Recovery -- This dive introduces students to basic underwater search patterns and recovery techniques. It must be made clear that this is not a public safety course, but an introduction to the use of basic patterns to locate lost objects of small size. The techniques and tools are suitable for locating things like fishing rods, boat motors, wallets, and other such items. The lift bags used should not exceed 100 lb capacity and smaller ones are preferred, with 25-50 lbs as an ideal size for lifting an object like a concrete block or bucket filled with weight. The use of a reel and line is required in order to execute a circular pattern and grid; it also serves as insurance should visibility be reduced by natural conditions or the actions of the searchers. The following skills are used in this dive:

a) Buoyancy control.

b) Selection of search pattern based on object size, approximate location, and environmental conditions.

c) Attention to terrain detail.

d) Maintaining trim and buoyancy while conducting a slow search using good anti-silting techniques with a buddy. Then, upon location of the object, taking a compass heading for future reference.

e) Securing the object to be lifted.

f) Lift bag use – Raise the object at a consistent rate, achieve neutral buoyancy with the bag,   bring the object to the surface, then return it to depth maintaining neutral buoyancy of both diver and object.

6. Buddy Skills and Assist – As the name implies, this dive reinforces proper buddy skills while introducing new skills that may be used to assist a dive buddy in need. Safety protocols are followed at all times while creating scenarios that nonetheless test and challenge students to deal with problems that may realistically arise on a dive. Mastering these skills increases confidence, situational awareness, and overall diver safety. With this in mind, the following scenarios can be used:

a) 100 foot no-mask swim.

b) 100 foot no-mask, air-share swim.

c) 100 foot no-mask, air-share swim and ascent.

d) Loss-of-buoyancy ascent/assist.

e) Bring up unconscious diver from depth (not to exceed 25 feet).

f) Rescue tow of unconscious diver.

These six dives make up the AOW class I offer. It can only be taken after the diver's basic skills have been evaluated by me prior to starting the class; if the diver's skills are in question, I will not allow them to begin advanced training until the skill deficits have been addressed. Few instructors offer a class such as this, but I have described it to give you an example of the subjects and skills an AOW class *can* contain. A good AOW class need not contain all the elements this one does, but it should contain some of them and offer new skills that will be useful on advanced dives.

As mentioned previously, some divers are not interested in or do not feel the need for what is taught in AOW, but are still interested and motivated for additional training of some kind. Other courses exist that can greatly benefit the diver without taking AOW, though agencies vary in their support of more customized diver education. Classes such as Underwater

Navigation, Nitrox, Dry Suit (for cold-water divers), and especially Rescue are highly beneficial, providing skills that can only improve diver comfort and safety. A good training regimen will take into account the diver's preferences at least as much as it accommodates the shop's schedule or agency's recommendations. A number of agencies empower the student and instructor to design or choose courses for a specific diver's development; it behooves students to carefully research the progression of training for each agency before signing up for courses. Some students may find that mixing course offerings from more than one agency is what best meets their needs. This is a perfectly acceptable practice, though students who do this need to be aware that the basic requirements vary by agency; training that meets the prerequisites for additional education in one agency may not do so for another.

To summarize, when choosing a course for training, you need to be very honest with yourself as you decide what you want to do. Agencies, shops, instructors, and specific courses all need to be carefully evaluated. If a course fails to meet your needs, this needs to be determined before the papers are signed and the course begun. It is easy enough to go online and find a world of information to use in evaluating training options. Any person or business offering a course should have enough pride and confidence in their material to support a potential student's desire to comparison-shop. If you are already Open Water certified and looking for further training, it is you -- not the agency, shop, or instructor -- who should have the final say in what that training will be. A dive professional's recommendations should be taken into account as you evaluate options, but you should never allow yourself to be talked into a course of questionable personal benefit. For those who are interested in further, more customized training, what follows is some basic information on the courses most often considered.

Specialty Courses

Nitrox is a course commonly chosen by new divers looking to expand their options. Nitrox (also called Enriched Air Nitrox) is the term given to air mixtures containing more than 21% oxygen. For recreational divers, it is commonly used to define mixtures containing up to 40% oxygen; oxygen content higher than 40% is usually reserved for technical divers. The majority of regulators on the market today are compatible with mixtures up to 40% oxygen with no additional modifications. Nitrox training is required due to the fact that when the oxygen content is increased, certain risks also increase. If you have taken an OW class, you have learned about gas laws and partial pressures. The partial pressure of oxygen in any gas mix will increase with depth. Oxygen becomes toxic at higher partial pressures, and the effect is cumulative across repetitive dives. In order to reduce this risk, there are depth restrictions and other calculations that must be made, which are not normally covered in the OW class.

As with so many other training courses, the content of many Nitrox courses has been reduced over time. Some now consist of little more than instruction to students in how analyze their tanks and set their computers for the proper gas mix before they are sent off with their new certifications to dive using Nitrox. Some instructors do not go through the calculations at all, or merely skim over them with the assumption that divers will only ever use either 32% or 36% Nitrox, the two most common mixes. Even though some dive operations bank one of these mixes, there is no guarantee that this is exactly what you will get; it can easily be off by one or two percent. While some may accept this, I do not. It is necessary not only to analyze every tank, but to also determine the Maximum Operating Depth (MOD) for every mix. One caution I would offer is that if you decide to take a Nitrox class, be sure that you need it. Nitrox is of little benefit for dives with depths of less than 50 feet, or if only doing two or three dives a day for a weekend. Where Nitrox comes into its own is on trips where multiple dives will be done over each of multiple days.

Some divers choose to dive with Nitrox in the belief that it is a safer option than air due to the lower nitrogen content. Nitrox only provides a margin of safety if your dives are the same length and depth as if you were using air. If you use Nitrox to extend your bottom time, as is commonly done, then your risk of decompression sickness (DCS) is the same. It is common practice, especially among older divers, to use Nitrox while diving plans based on air tables or while using a computer set for air. Using Nitrox this way does increase safety by reducing the amount of nitrogen exposure; the less nitrogen you absorb in the first place, the less you have to get rid of.

Underwater Navigation is another excellent course for overall diver development that can be taken without the AOW class. A good course in underwater navigation will reinforce buddy skills, enhance communication skills, and aid divers in developing their ability to work as a team. It will also require divers to work on buoyancy and trim -- always a good thing. Perhaps the most important benefit of an Underwater Navigation class though, is that it increases a diver's comfort and confidence in the water, thereby improving that diver's safety. As you develop the ability to set a course, swim that course, and then return to the starting point with less effort each time, this builds a sense of accomplishment and increased confidence not only in your skills, but in yourself. This ability is one of the hallmarks of an accomplished diver; I believe it is a core skill that should be developed, and that any diver will benefit from doing so. Successful navigation requires attention to detail and, by necessity, reduced speed. This will have the fortunate side benefit of helping the new diver to slow down and more fully enjoy the dive. In my own experience, it has allowed me to see things I may otherwise have missed. Small objects and animals are much easier to spot when swimming at a nice, relaxed pace instead of rushing around trying to see everything. Another real plus is that for the diver who has no desire to go deep, the Underwater Navigation course can and should be done in relatively shallow water that will allow plenty of time to practice the new skills. Like the AOW class, the Underwater Navigation class should also include some classroom time to go over techniques, equipment, and hazards, as well as the benefits of acquiring these skills. When researching the available options for taking this class, it is important to compare the course content of several different instructors to assure that you ultimately get what you most want from taking it.

As you can see, the classes available beyond OW are not all the same. There are major differences that simply cannot be overlooked when choosing a training path. The more time you spend researching and comparing classes, the better off you will be. When you get down to it, further training is all about what will be best for *you*. It is about whatever best enhances your safety and enjoyment of the sport. Speaking of enjoyment, there are courses you can take purely for the enhancement of that part of your diving experience, as you'll see next.

Underwater Photography is a popular course as it gives us the opportunity to share our experiences with those who do not dive. It also is a way to preserve memories for ourselves. I look back through some of the photos I have taken over the years and am reminded of some great times and experiences: On the sand, lying next to a nurse shark under a ledge while taking a picture of it; a doorway into the depths of the Spiegel Grove; looking out the portholes from inside a compartment on the Duane; looking out over an expanse of reef with some very cool coral formations. These are just a few of my own special memories that are preserved in photographs, but as much as they mean to me, I do not teach an Underwater Photography course. As much as I enjoy the photos, I am not passionate about the art of taking them, nor am I passionate about knowing every fish on a reef.

My belief is that for a student to get all they can out of one of these courses, they need to find someone who *is* passionate about it. There are several instructors I refer students to for courses in underwater (UW) photography. These instructors are not only passionate about the subject, but actually make a living at it. They have been published in national magazines, online, and in books. They are the ones who will give the student a course of the quality that I would want for myself. Some UW Photography specialties can be offered by instructors who have simply attended a one-day workshop. While the information gained in such workshops is undoubtedly useful, it cannot take the place of experience and practice in structuring a comprehensive course. Find an instructor who can show you published works and who knows how to get the most out of your camera setup. Don't take a course that has been designed to sell you a new camera or give you a new plastic card. You do not need another card to buy or rent a camera, or to take a camera on a dive. Some of the best UW Photography classes offer no additional certification at all; what they offer is knowledge, skill, and great results.

Fish Identification is best taken from someone who is passionate about that subject. There are instructors who are also marine biologists, who really *know* what they are talking about. They incorporate fish identification with reef ecology, impacts of invasive species and man on the environment, and know the habits of various animals. There are also instructors who, while not scientists, are passionate about the subject and will spend significant time on research and documenting their sightings. Try to find a course taught by one of these two kinds of instructors. Using myself as an example again, I do not teach a course in fish identification, because it is not my passion. I could buy a book and learn a lot of stuff about fish. I could then charge a nice sum for certifying students in fish identification by sharing my newly-gained book knowledge. But students could buy the same book on their own and probably learn more for a lot less money! Offering a course like this would be shortchanging the student, in my view. In short, choose carefully when deciding on these types of courses. Some are set up primarily to generate income for those who offer them. Others are offered by conscientious instructors who are passionate about the subject and have developed it to new levels; find one of them before taking the plunge into any type of training in areas like this.

Equipment Maintenance doesn't even require time in the water but is extremely valuable for divers who plan on diving locally or who travel a great deal with their own equipment. Not to be confused with factory service courses for technicians who actually tear down and repair gear, the maintenance course covers the basics of taking care of your gear beyond what may have been discussed in the Open Water class. These classes, like the others, are not all created equal. Some are more comprehensive and cover subjects like tank inspections; unless you have your own compressor, that is good general information to have, but is not really necessary. The maintenance I am talking about involves the hands-on repairs and upkeep likely to be needed by any diver at some point, like how to replace a hose, replacing or repairing a dump valve on a BC, or changing an O-ring. It might also include changing the HP spool on an SPG; this is a simple repair once you know how, which could save a dive day or even an entire trip. You'll need to learn about proper lubrication of the O-rings on any lights or cameras that you carry -- too little lube and they can dry out and crack, too much and they will accumulate dirt than can cause a failure. A good course will help you find that fine line in the middle that works. There might be some content on the repair/maintenance of exposure suits, since some problems that come up do not require the return of the suit to the dive shop or manufacturer. Adding thigh pockets, for example, can be done at home with Aquaseal, a couple large books, some weights, cardboard, and a colored pencil or tailor's chalk. A loose thread can easily be repaired and extend the life of an expensive wet suit. Even adding a P-valve to a dry suit need not be feared, although intentionally putting a hole into a $1000 suit always causes you to hesitate and even question your sanity! Your maintenance course should include information on what items you need to keep on hand to facilitate common repairs, along with other items needed to thwart common dive-day problems (spare fin strap, etc.). The course should also include a section on optimal equipment selection. A good course can be done in four to six hours; a great one may take a little longer and go into more detail. Either way, this information can and has saved many dives for untold numbers of divers.

This chapter will end with a reminder of some key points. When deciding on training, consider what you ultimately want -- do you want to be able to dive independently, or do you want just enough training to manage as long as you have supervision? Research the standards of the various certifying agencies to determine which ones meet your requirements. Choose an instructor as previously described, and select courses based on content and comprehensiveness of training. Make sure that you are offered the time and attention necessary to meet your needs while satisfying agency or shop standards.

Finally, you might ask yourself, "Just how much do I want to be capable of doing?" I have two requirements for evaluating student competency at the completion of a course. Before I hand a student a certification card, I ask myself two questions: "Would I be okay with this person as my buddy?" and, "Would I trust this person to dive with my son, daughter, or other loved one with no dive professional present?" When the answer to both questions is yes, I hand them their card. If there was ever any doubt, I would determine why and we would address that before certification was granted. That has yet to happen, which reflects as much on the dedication and thirst for knowledge of my students as it does on my instructional methods.

Along with determining a training path and finding an instructor, it would be remiss of me not to include a section on choosing a dive shop. Your local dive shop is a major source of equipment, training, and even travel for divers. As with all else in SCUBA training, there is wide variation in the quality of dive shops you will encounter, so the next section will include information to help you sort out your options.

Notes

Chapter Ten
Choosing a Dive Shop

The local dive shop is often the first point of contact for people wishing to learn to SCUBA dive, though that has changed to some degree thanks to the Internet. Divers can buy equipment online and book trips. You can locate independent instructors via our websites. You can even get some of your training on the Internet. For most divers, however, nothing can replace the dive shop as the primary resource for these various needs, as well as for air fills. You already know that the earliest divers in the US did not have the benefit of dedicated gear vendors, and sometimes even had to build their own equipment. That has all changed thanks to the dive shop, which not only sells gear, but often also provides training, sets up clubs, organizes dives, and books trips to exotic or not-so-exotic places. Over the years the shops, equipment, and methods of selling (online sales) have evolved with the rest of society, but the basic concept is still the same: The dive shop is a one-stop place for divers to train and equip themselves. This is generally very beneficial, but it does have its drawbacks.

Early on, equipment choices were very limited; few companies manufactured SCUBA equipment. That has changed dramatically, which is a very good thing. Numerous companies now make excellent equipment. Unfortunately, the dive shop is highly unlikely to be able to carry every brand. Whether it is the size of the shop or policies of some manufacturers to limit competition, only the largest retailer can carry more than a few brands, which may have the effect of limiting your choice of equipment. While nearly all equipment is suitable for use in most dive environments, some is better suited to certain individuals based on their specific needs. This can be due to cost, style, availability of service in other areas, or just because you want a particular brand you have researched and feel is best for you. In addition to equipment issues, the instruction offered can vary greatly from shop to shop. Some shops have instructors on staff and the shop decides which instructor gets a class. This can result in a situation where your personality does not mesh with that of the instructor. On the other hand, it relieves you of having to select an instructor, which can be convenient. The dive shop is about convenience in many ways. It takes time and money to research a variety of resources to find the best one for equipment, the best one for instruction, and the best one for travel information. It is great when you can have all these needs met in a professional and courteous manner in one place, with your best interests in mind. Sometimes that happens, but experience shows that is not always the case.

I have dealt with shops that were models of how to meet the needs of the student first and foremost. I have also dealt with others where the primary focus was clearly on profit, and student needs were secondary. Fortunately, I've seen a number of shops that meet the needs of the student and do it well while still turning a nice profit, or at least managing to stay in business. So how do you choose a dive shop that will put your needs first, yet still make enough money to be there in the future when you want to go back for more training, to buy more gear, or to get service on gear you already own? In much the same way as you choose an instructor -- evaluate, compare, and talk with other divers. Evaluating a dive shop is a bit different than interviewing an instructor, however. Part of the evaluation process is the first impression you get when walking into the shop itself. An important tip here is to not use that first impression – positive or negative – as your only criterion in deciding whether the shop is a good one. A shop with a bit of clutter, a few items waiting to be stocked, and a little musty smell may be a far better choice than the one that is spotlessly clean, brightly lit, and has an aroma of fresh carpet. The first shop's owner may choose to spend all of his extra cash on keeping a good inventory, while the other may have much on display but need to order the item you want. Or it could be just the opposite. The point is that first impression of the facility can be misleading. The first impression that matters more is that of the staff, even though the staff may just be one or two people. Most dive shops are run by just one or two regular employees, one of whom is usually the owner. These employees can give a new diver a good feel for the type of diver the shop produces. If it is the owner, he or she may also be the chief (or only) instructor for the shop. Sometimes the owner is not an instructor but has one or more on staff, or uses several independent contract instructors. Whichever the case, this is a good time to begin the interview process. If the employee is also the instructor, go through the instructor interview as a start. Follow this with some or all of the following questions:

1. *"How long have you been in business?"* Remember that a brand new shop is not a bad thing; staff are likely to be up on all the latest trends and have the latest equipment. On the other hand, they have not yet developed much of a track record, so it may be harder to determine the customer service and instructional values they really practice.

2. *"What brands do you regularly carry and do you service them in-house?"* Equipment service is a necessary part of owning SCUBA gear. You do not want to be waiting three or four weeks to get a regulator serviced because the shop had to send it out.

3. *"If I have a brand that you don't carry, can you service it or tell me where to get it serviced?"* Shops that will work with a student on this often do much better than those who try to sell the student something carried in-house. The referral to get a regulator serviced elsewhere may result in a future sale for the shop if the student decides that going somewhere else is too inconvenient.

4. *"If I want an item that you don't have in stock or a brand that you don't carry, can you get it or will you refer me to somewhere that I can get it?"* Smart shops try to obtain the items a student wants, or will refer them elsewhere as needed. Again, a willingness to truly help the student will result in good will and a positive reputation than could never be achieved through paid advertising.

91

5. *"What agency or agencies do you offer certification through?"* Some may tell you that at the Open Water level, this is not a big deal. Remember though, that there are wide differences in requirements and course content among different agencies. Use the answer to this question to research whether the agency or agencies named match your requirements.

6. *"Can I choose my instructor?"* This is important. Remember that they are working for you. Even if the instructor is a shop employee, you are still paying them to train you.

7. *"Where do you hold classes?"* Some shops have on-site pools and classrooms. Others use locations that may be a bit of a drive. This is not a deal breaker but should be determined before signing up for the class.

8. *"Who sets the class schedule?"* Ideally, you should determine when you can train but if the shop is renting classroom or pool space, they may not be able to offer this option. It then falls on you to make time in their schedule for training. While the shop and instructor do work for you, there must be some commitment and compromise on your part to train as necessary.

9. *"How big are the classes?"* While large classes can be a sign of a successful shop and good instruction, they may also indicate a lack of sufficient time for students to practice what they have learned. In general, smaller classes leave time for more individualized instruction that often results in better trained and more competent divers.

10. *"Are your instructors allowed to give more time to individual students if they need it?"* This is another very important issue. It should be up to you and the instructor to determine your needs, and to determine when you are ready for checkout dives. These decisions should never be in the hands of anyone not directly involved with your training (even if it's the shop owner).

11. *"What items are included in the costs of the class?"* No grey area here. It should be clear at the beginning – preferably

in writing -- what each party is responsible for and the various costs involved.

12. *"What type of rental equipment do you have and will it be what I use for my checkout dives?"* This is not a major issue, but it is nice if the gear used on checkouts is the same or similar to that which was used in the pool training.

13. *"Do you offer local diving opportunities?"* Local diving is where skills are developed and refined. Local diving allows students to practice and work on techniques while not breaking the bank for airfare, resort costs, etc.

14. *"What types of trips do you offer?"* Shops that plan and take a number of trips usually have larger pools of divers that might be willing to buddy up with a new person.

15. *"Do you support or recommend any dive clubs?"* Club activities are a great source of dive opportunities and new buddies. Be careful though, as a club that is sponsored or supported by a shop is somewhat beholden to that shop. This can cause issues when a club member shows up with new equipment the shop does not carry, or with a new certification from an instructor not affiliated with the shop. These issues are eliminated with fully independent clubs.

16. *"Do you offer discounts on equipment and trips to students and regular customers?"* This is another way that successful shops keep customers and attract new students. They work within a competitive market to earn the loyalty of their local dive community.

17. *"May I have the names of divers you have trained, as references?"* The successful shop should easily and happily meet this request.

18. *"What sets you apart from other shops that would make me want to train with you?"* I'll leave the correct answer up to you to determine, based on the knowledge you have gained so far.

What I have listed above are questions that I would ask when selecting a dive shop. You may have additional questions of your own to add to this list, or you may not feel the need to ask all of these. Other factors such as shop location, location of checkout dives, and the climate where the shop is located may raise other issues you will need to clarify. I am certain by this point that if you have read all of the information in this book, you are capable of deciding the other questions you need to ask.

The next factor you should consider when choosing a dive shop is the divers that they turn out. Do the shop's customers come in and just hang out to socialize and talk? The most active, popular shops I have frequented rarely go a full day without someone just stopping in to say hi or to window-shop. When divers like and trust their dive shop, they spend time there. Sometimes it is to buy equipment, while other times it is to get information or just share some camaraderie with other divers. Pay attention to the attitude of the divers who hang out at the shop. Are they friendly or do there seem to be cliques that are stand-offish? This does not mean all the divers they train will be like this but it can be an indication of the attitudes of the owner and instructors; this may need to be considered when planning an outing or trip with them.

The shop should have a "Welcome, friend," feel to it. This is different than walking onto a used car lot where they immediately assume you need to buy something. The dive shop staff should be friendly and helpful, yet not pushy. I do not expect an employee to drop everything he or she is doing and rush over to me. In fact, that is one sure way to get me to never come in again. I *do* expect a hello and "How are you?" If the employee adds that if I need any help to just ask, that's okay but not required. The staff should know what they are talking about; it helps if they themselves dive. When you ask about equipment, the staff should know the product. They should know how it works, why it is suitable for you and more importantly, whether there is a better alternative based on your specific needs. They should be able to explain the choices you have as those choices relate to *your* needs, interests, and means. Finally, though they need not wear a suit and tie, the staff should come across as knowledgeable and professional. When you ask a question, you should get an answer that makes sense. It is perfectly acceptable to hear, "I don't know," or, "I'm not sure." That should immediately be followed by, "But I will find out!" It is better to hear that than to waste time listening to someone try to explain something they really don't understand.

The dive shop can be one of the most important sources of information and service to the diver, but beware. It can also be a bottomless pit that swallows your money if you get hooked on good training and great deals on gear!

©2006 James A Lapenta -- To below decks on the Spiegel Grove

Notes

Chapter Eleven
Gear Selection and Your Dive Shop

You might look at the array of equipment available at your local dive shop and wonder how that particular inventory came to be chosen. Clearly, the owner chooses how to stock the store, but the owner does not enjoy the full independence in this decision-making that you might assume. Some of the owner's choices will be personal preference, while some will be a reflection of the particular market that shop serves, and still others will be essentially forced on the owner by gear manufacturers.

It is common to walk into a dive shop for the first time and feel overwhelmed at all the choices and types of equipment on display. The first thing to realize is that the apparently dizzying variety is somewhat misleading. There seem to be so many different versions of everything, yet closer inspection often reveals that all of this variety is from one, two, or perhaps three manufacturers for the "big ticket" items like BCs and regulators. There may be some smaller or specialty items from other lines, but generally a shop picks up one or two major lines and builds the inventory around those. Customers are then often limited to equipment made by those manufacturers when it comes time to purchase their gear from that shop.

This is not generally a problem, as the equipment from every major manufacturer is safe and will do the job. It becomes an issue when the stocked lines do not meet your needs. It may be that the lines are too expensive, do not fit properly, or are just not the style you want. It may be possible for the shop to get other merchandise that does meet your needs, but the cost may be higher or there may be a long wait time for the order to come in; sometimes, the shop may be unable to get the item at all. At this point, you need to make a decision that can have a negative effect on your relationship with the dive shop – you may have to go elsewhere to get what you really want. No one likes to lose a sale, and some shop owners are more upset about doing so than others.

When a diver does make a choice to go elsewhere, who is to blame for the dive shop losing that sale? The shop? The diver? The answer may be neither. It may actually be a manufacturer, whether or not that manufacturer's gear is carried by the shop. The manufacturer whose gear the dive shop carries may limit the ability of the shop to bring in competing gear. The manufacturer not normally carried by the shop may refuse to sell a single item to someone who has no dealer arrangement with them. It is likely all good equipment with a solid reputation, so some manufacturers go to great lengths to limit competition with their products in the shops that sell their lines. They may have policies that restrict the number of other lines the shop may carry and how much space is allowed for other lines in the shop. The dive shop is often required to maintain a set inventory level and to place orders for minimum amounts that, if not maintained, may result in the downgrading or loss of their dealer status. Manufacturers can prevent the dealer from offering sales without prior approval, prohibit Internet sales, and set limits on in-store promotions. It should be noted that these business practices are not at all specific to the SCUBA industry, but are especially visible here. These same measures are in play in most retail settings, right down to your local grocery store.

Even a shop's geographic location may come into play when manufacturers decide who will get dealership contracts and who will not. In an area like the Florida Keys, you may be able to find three shops within a mile of each other all carrying the same brand. Because there are so many potential customers and the prices are controlled due to dealer agreements, the competition is based on the quality of service and instruction offered. In locations with less traffic, such as a small town in the Midwest, the manufacturer may not allow shops within five to ten miles of each other to compete with the same lines. Several manufacturers offer a secondary line that, while of the same general quality, has fewer features or features that are less expensive to produce. They sometimes award their primary line to one dealer, while making the secondary line available to a competing dealer in close range.

The SCUBA industry is unique in some ways when it comes to merchandising rules and practices. Several sporting goods chains have a SCUBA section but it is not their primary business, and some manufacturers prefer not to deal with large chains not devoted to diving. They prefer to keep the sales of gear in the hands of the people most likely to train the customer in the use of that gear. This is good for diver safety, but is carried out in a manner that greatly restricts both consumer choice and dealer freedom.

Ideally, a retailer could buy an item from a manufacturer or distributor, figure in some overhead expense, and then set a price for the item that covers costs and allows for some profit. In the SCUBA industry, some gear manufacturers deny dealers this freedom. Dealers may be told what prices they must use, which will be described in more detail in Chapter 12. Dealers must carefully consider which gear line(s) to carry, having to balance the relative risks of which manufacturers they'll have to answer to and which manufacturers may exclude them from ordering altogether. In addition, dealers have to assure that what they choose will be accepted by their customers; if a line carries high MSRPs, for example, new divers may balk at the expense. Having balanced all the risks and needs to choose certain manufacturers to represent, dealers then naturally feel some pressure to sell the gear they have chosen to carry in order to stay in business. What they recommend to students may be the students' best choice given what is available through the shop, but it may not be the best available fit for some students' needs. Dealers may insist that what they carry is better than any other brand or is of higher quality. Students may even be required to use this gear in order to participate in training or other shop-sponsored activities. Shops may exert even stronger control with their students who decide to develop themselves as dive professionals. Those students may be required not only to use the gear their shop sells, but to use only the most expensive pieces of that equipment. They may be required to update the entire setup every year or two. Sometimes they are offered a deal that may include trading in the old equipment and getting the new at what are known as "key-man" prices. These deals are offered to certain shop employees who are of high value to the operation. The savings are great, but may still not justify the divemaster or instructor having to spend additional money to replace perfectly good gear. They'll have to spend the money anyway though, because if they wish to continue working for the shop, they must have this new equipment. This is done in the belief that students will see the "pros" using this gear, and will think they also must have it.

It might seem that the dive shop could solve these conflict-of-interest issues simply by choosing to carry only gear from manufacturers without restrictive business practices, then hand-selecting only the very best offerings from each line, but even this isn't necessarily true. Dealers can get in over their heads with numerous lines that offer too much of a selection. Variety is good, but too much of it can confuse students and reduce the profit margin of the shop. Another reason that shops may not carry a multitude of lines is that when they carry just one or two lines, the staff knows those lines very well. They know how those lines work, why they work, what they can and cannot do, and best of all, they can fix problems that may arise. Service and maintenance of equipment also plays into what lines the shop decides to carry. For each line, the shop must maintain an inventory of parts, service kits, and manuals. Many small shops simply lack the physical space to adequately service more than a line or two. In addition, the dealer will have to attend service clinics in order to stay up-to-date with gear offered in the shop; the clinics are often free or nearly so, but still involve the time and expense of travel. Many are not able to afford the added cost just to stay current on a line from which they may only make one or two sales in a year.

This all said, there are some shops that can carry numerous lines of equipment successfully, service them all competently, and still make enough profit to keep the doors open. They are located in large areas with high traffic, they use the Internet very successfully to sell SCUBA equipment to customers around the world... and they are the exception. The norm is the small, independent shop that cannot carry more than two or three lines. So how do they choose what lines to carry?

The smart shop owner looks at his potential clientele and the conditions in which they most often dive, then chooses what merchandise to carry, based on their needs. For example, a Caribbean shop owner will not bring in an extensive line of dry suits or cold-water regulators, but those items had better be in plentiful supply in a Minnesota shop. Shops near good wreck diving will have a nice selection of technical gear and the accessories that tech diving requires. Shops near deep inland quarries and lakes tend to carry more recreationally oriented lines, but would also do well to carry a tech line in addition. New divers should not rule out "tech" equipment for their first set of gear. They may have an interest in going down that path in the future, but even if they don't, it is still good equipment for recreational diving.

As you can see, many factors go into determining what gear choices you have when you go into your local dive shop. A good dealer will be willing to explain honestly why they carry brand X over brand Y. If they say it's because brand Y is junk, be wary. No major brand is junk. This is the time to take a step back and do some research from independent sources such as message boards and customer reviews of specific items. Gear reviews appear in dive magazines, but the caution here is that the review may be based simply on what gear the manufacturer sent to the reviewer, and may be subject to bias. For more comprehensive and balanced information, look for reviews that are based on independently purchased, competing items.

As noted previously, all shops and instructors are not created equal. Some truly excel at prioritizing the needs of the student. If we were able to go to a big-box, general-merchandise chain store we would very likely get a good deal on gear. It is also likely that the person selling that gear would have no idea how it is properly used, let alone be able to train the purchaser in its use. In my opinion, this would result in many more divers and wannabe divers getting killed by improper use of equipment. There is nothing preventing someone with enough money from buying all the necessary equipment to dive -- including a compressor for filling tanks -- and going diving. This was, in fact, how many started SCUBA in the early days of the sport. When you go into a dive shop and look at the equipment displayed there, you must consider the fact that the person behind the counter most likely (though not always) knows what they are talking about. This is a factor of great value that must also be considered when you are judging the fairness of the price you ultimately pay for your gear.

To summarize, do some research before buying the first item your dive shop recommends. Compare prices and brands. Look at features *you* feel you will need. Ask dive shop staff why they carry the brands they do. Ask if there are equivalent items out there, and how they compare in value. If you are told the alternatives are not as good a value, ask how the dealer has reached this conclusion. What features or extras make the dealer's line better? What will be the result if you do not want or cannot afford to buy their line? Will going elsewhere affect your ability to train with them? Frankly, it should not. Finally, if you really have your heart set on a piece of gear they do not carry, give them the opportunity to get it or a comparable item before going elsewhere. They may not be aware that the item is on the market or know the manufacturer; new manufacturers come up all the time and it is difficult for shop staff to be familiar with all of them. You may in fact be doing them a favor by making them aware of the new guy on the block. If they still do not want or are not able to get what you request, don't settle for something you don't really want. It's your dive, your plan, your equipment. You are the one who will have to use it for a long time to come. By all means, give the local dive shop a chance, but not at the expense of your personal comfort, goals, means, and perhaps, safety.

Chapter Twelve
Equipment Options and Information

New and newer divers have many questions when it comes to dive equipment. Ideally, many such questions are answered in initial training by the instructor. I receive so many of these questions from my website, via e-mail, phone, and in the form of private messages on the forums I frequent, however, that it appears students are not getting the answers they need. The questions concern basic issues like the minimum gear the diver should own or what type of BC or regulator is the best choice. They ask about cost and even use of the equipment. An entire book could be written on all the gear that is available and within weeks, be outdated. What I am going to do in this chapter is cover the basics as I see them and those add-ons, which while not truly required, make diving safer and more enjoyable. I have my own preferences as to types and manufacturers, but will refrain from recommending any one brand.

It is my hope that with good Open Water training, this will serve as a generic guide to more informed choices, equipping new divers to do the personal research that helps them decide what is best for them. We'll just start now with the mask, snorkel, fins, and boots and go from there into the other areas.

Masks

Masks are perhaps the most important part of the diver's kit. Necessary to see with and for equalization, it is impossible to dive without one. There are dozens of styles to choose from; nearly every major SCUBA manufacturer markets a mask. What is not commonly known is that, with limited exceptions, there are only three or four makers of masks in the world. They are located in Southeast Asia and make masks for a number of companies. The only real difference is a logo that the company puts on the mask for sale to the diver. A little research will have the diver finding his or her mask being sold by several companies under different brands, and at sometimes substantially different prices. It pays to shop around. As I hope you know, the two most important qualities in a mask are comfort and fit. Everything else truly is secondary.

The mask that is sold by Premium Dive Company X may also be marketed by Not-So-Premium Dive Company Y and at less cost. Same mask, same fit, less expense to the diver. Manufacturers may also offer quantity discounts to shops that can result in substantial savings to the consumer. The Dive Equipment & Marketing Association (DEMA) has a trade show every year that is only open to shops, resorts, and dive professionals. It is held in November and at this show, the equipment manufacturers will offer deals to shops. Sometimes these deals are on new products coming out, on older products that are being phased out, on overstocks, or all of the above. Shops place orders for these items for immediate delivery in the case of older products or overstocks, and as preorders for the new products. Chances are if the shop has a large selection at Christmas or in the first part of the year on masks (or any other item), it is a result of one of these deals and you may be able to get a better price than what it is usually sold for. Don't be afraid to haggle and ask for a better deal. A good shop owner may realize that the small cut he takes now on a mask could lead to much a much bigger sale later on.

But let's get back to the mask itself. No matter how much or how little one pays for a mask, if it does not fit properly and is not comfortable, it is junk -- for that diver. A soft skirt that molds to the face is a must, along with a tempered glass lens. Some masks sold at sporting goods or retail stores may have silicone skirts, but the material is not as soft as that found on dive shop masks. Mass market masks are designed for snorkeling where one would not typically wear a mask as long as a diver would; in most cases, such masks are a very poor choice for SCUBA diving. When choosing a mask, along with comfort and fit, I look to see if it is high volume, low volume, or somewhere in between. The volume of a mask refers to the size of the air space between the lens and the diver's face. A low volume mask typically sits closer, has a lower overall profile (reducing drag), and is less likely to have peripheral windows on the sides. While peripheral windows do offer some increase in the field of the diver's vision, a low profile mask has the same effect because of less skirt material at the sides. The low profile also reduces the amount of air needed to clear the mask. For some, however, the low profile mask may present a problem due to it being so close to the face. Those divers with prominent brows or noses may find a low profile mask uncomfortable. Again, comfort and fit are the primary concerns and a properly trained diver can clear a high volume mask as easily as a low volume one.

Next is the lens itself -- single window or double lens design? I have both and frankly see little if any difference. Underwater, the difference between single and double lens is like regular glasses in that there *is* no difference; the "line" between the lenses disappears and we see one continuous visual field, the same as on land. One advantage is that a double lens design more easily allows for the installation of prescription lenses, though they can be bonded to the inside of a single lens if necessary.

The water, as you know, makes objects appear closer and larger. For some divers, that magnification is still not enough to be able to comfortably read gauges and see small objects or critters of interest. Magnification in SCUBA mask lenses can be accomplished in a number of ways. Many manufacturers offer drop-in lenses that magnify to the desired level. There are also small plastic-like inserts that adhere to the lower part of the lens, which can be used many times -- a poor man's bifocal, if you will. Then there are companies that will take a diver's actual prescription (including bifocals) and grind tempered lenses to fit the mask. Some replace the mask lenses (in the case of some double lens masks), while others are bonded to the inside of the existing lens or lenses, depending on mask type. My only issue with dive mask prescription lenses is that they make my land lenses look like they were done by amateurs! The vision quality of the lenses I have is really that good. They are expensive, but well worth it for those who will use a mask regularly.

A final consideration for some is the matter of a purge valve. Located in the nose pocket, a purge valve is said to allow the diver to clear the mask more easily because it does not require the diver to tilt the head back. In fact, masks with a purge are actually tilted down to allow the water to accumulate in the nose; by simply holding the mask to the face and exhaling through the nose, water is forced out the valve. Snorkelers also like them as they do not have to lift their heads out of the water to clear. One caution though is that some divers have difficulty equalizing with a purge mask due to the valve location. It is at the end of the nose pocket and can sometimes interfere with pinching the nose (as is done with the Valsalva maneuver) and becomes more of an issue if the diver is wearing thick gloves. It is not a major issue, but an issue that should be noted before spending money on a mask like this. In most cases, a purge valve does not and should not add to the cost of the mask. It should be remembered though, that nothing will replace proper technique and practice for clearing a mask.

Snorkels

Snorkels are a somewhat contentious item of the SCUBA kit. Some divers insist on them, some despise them as unnecessary, and some -- like me -- are somewhere in the middle of the debate. A snorkel is a tube to carry air when you want to keep your face in the water and not use the SCUBA regulator. Underwater, on SCUBA, it has no use. It hangs there next to the inflator and is sometimes mistaken for it, or vice versa. In certain environments, it is even a hazard; it can get tangled in kelp, fishing line, etc. and result in the mask being pulled from the diver's face. It has limited use at the surface considering that if conditions are bad enough to require it, the diver should just use the regulator. On the other hand, a snorkel is very useful when conditions are good and a surface swim to the descent point will preserve more tank air for the dive. It used to be taught that a snorkel could be used in rescue situations to deliver air to an unconscious diver. The fact is that the snorkels most often sold to divers today are utterly useless for that purpose because of the lower exhaust diaphragm. While features like dry valves, semi-dry baffle systems, or an extra-large diameter bore may be nice for snorkeling, they are not ideal choices for SCUBA diving. I prefer what is known as a pocket snorkel with a quick-release clip. Offered by several companies in different versions, a pocket snorkel is easily detached from the mask and can be stored in a BC pocket. Available if necessary, yet out of the way otherwise, they are perhaps the best option, offering all of the advantages of a snorkel with none of the inconveniences or hazards. It should be noted that they still have the lower diaphragm which prevents their use for rescue breathing.

Still in use by free divers and available from a number of online retailers are the old fashioned "J" tube snorkels. Updated with the latest in materials and also foldable when not in use, these would be my next choice. They tend to be less expensive than the ones with all the gimmicks sold in dive shops. Contrary to what some marketing campaigns would have you believe, they are no harder for the properly trained diver to clear than any other snorkel. In short, simple is best. There is no reason to spend $30 or more on a snorkel. None. Take the savings and get a better quality mask, boots, or fins.

Boots

Boots and fins are the next items to consider as part of your basic gear. There are divers who use full foot fins without boots, but they are not quite as common. I'm going to concentrate on what is most often sold and used among new and newer divers, with a nod to those of us who are not so new. The most common style of fin marketed to new divers is the open heel fin that is used with a neoprene boot. The boot is an integral part of this system as it helps to reduce chafing on the foot and heel, keeps the fin somewhat steadier on the foot, and is extremely useful when walking on surfaces at a dive site that would be less than friendly to bare feet. Boots also reduce the chance of slipping on a wet boat deck and reduce the risk of injury should one's foot come into contact with an errant, solid lead weight.

Boots are available in a variety of styles from a basic low-cut slipper to ones that look like they could go into combat; most are somewhere in between. Important features to look for include good tread design and adequate insulation. Boots should also be easy to get on and off. Many have zippers that run up the side, but some are made of stretchable materials that simply slip on. Another good feature to look for is a puncture-resistant sole. Important for very rocky areas or where sharp objects such as broken glass or perhaps sea urchins may be encountered, this feature has saved many divers' feet. Finally, the most important consideration with boots, as with your other gear, is comfort and fit.

Fins

Fins are usually divided into two types – paddle and split. They each have their own distinct advantages, so you must choose whatever works best for your individual needs. Paddle fins are often chosen for power. Split fins tend to be easier on the knees and ankles. Fins can be purchased new for prices ranging from about $50 up to nearly $300; there is even a fin that costs over $800! Cost generally reflects different materials (rubber, plastic, exotic composites), strap types, and in some cases, the brand name. For the beginning diver, it really does not matter what style of fin you choose. Chances are you will, at some point, replace it or at least try something different. When choosing an entry level fin, look for good, solid construction. It should have some flex, yet not be too floppy. Power comes from the fin being able to flex and return to its original shape. SCUBA fins tend to be much larger than those typically sold for snorkeling; they need to be in order to propel a fully geared diver through the water.

A critical part of the fin is the strap. Usually made of rubber, it holds the fin on the foot by means of buckles that allow the strap to be lengthened or shortened as needed. The only problem with rubber straps is that they can and do break. Age, a defect in the rubber, a small cut -- any of these can cause a strap to fail. Many divers have chosen to replace their rubber straps with stainless steel springs which are less likely to break, more comfortable, and easier to doff and don.

These four items (mask, snorkel, fins, and boots) make up the basic equipment package divers are expected to have for their checkout dives. Some instructors and shops require students to own these items before class actually starts; my own students just need to have this gear before checkouts. Until then, they may bring personal gear they already have, purchase the items at the shop where I teach, purchase them elsewhere, or borrow the gear provided at the pool. Now that you are equipped to make some economical and appropriate purchases of your basic gear, we'll go over those other items you are most likely to purchase.

Exposure Suits

The next item a diver purchases after basic gear is often some type of exposure protection, but what kind? It depends on a number of factors such as water temperature, duration of dives, and surface air temperatures. Exposure suits come in a variety of colors. Dark colors are more often represented for several reasons: Dark colors are less likely to show dirt, retain heat more than lighter ones, and some believe that darker colors just look cool. Many custom colors are available for those who want them. Exposure suits can be wet suits, dry suits, or semi-dry suits. The most common is the wet suit.

Wet Suits

Usually made of neoprene, the function of the suit is to slow the amount of heat lost while diving. Called a wet suit because of the layer of water that is trapped between it and the skin, these suits come in various thicknesses and with many different features. Wet suits can range from .5 millimeter (mil) thickness which is appropriate for the tropics, to the 7 mil thick suits used in cold-water diving. Wet suits are also used in layers to maximize their thermal properties. A common way of doing this is with what is known as a Farmer John or Farmer Jane style suit. As illustrated below, the farmer style suit is a two-piece suit with a long-sleeve top and short legs, over sleeveless overall pants. A hooded diver wearing this suit has excellent thermal protection while also having the option of wearing either part alone. If this were a 7 mil thickness, the total thickness over the torso (core) would be 14 mil.

Note that not only can the two pieces be used separately or together, they can also be coupled with other components of differing thickness for a truly versatile system. It is entirely possible to buy several different thicknesses of either component and have a system that can be used for every condition from warm-water, tropical destinations to some of the coldest. When doing this, it is even possible to mix components from different manufacturers to achieve the best protection for the diver. As with most gear, fit and comfort are primary considerations.

The full wet suit is a one piece unit. Made in either front or back zip, from .5 mil to 7 mil thickness, the one piece suit is popular with many divers. It can also be layered with a vest or shortie suit to increase its warmth.

A wet suit, whether it is one piece or two, should fit snugly to minimize water movement between the suit and the diver. Water trapped in the suit is part of what keeps the diver warm and when the water flows through, a lot of heat goes with it. The suit must, however, not be so tight as to restrict circulation or drastically hinder movement. The thicker the suit, the warmer it will be, and the harder it will be to move in it. When choosing a suit, a good rule of thumb is to buy a suit based on the coldest temperatures the diver is likely to encounter. This is even more important if the diver plans on buying only one suit. Many divers own two or more suits and choose between them, based on where they will be diving and what the water and air temperatures will be. Temperature tolerance is one of those factors that differ with every diver when it comes to choosing a suit. What may be enough for one diver may be totally inadequate for another. It really is a matter of experience when it comes to selecting the proper suit. Divers will often rent different suits before buying one, to determine what style and thickness best meet their individual needs.

When you do decide to purchase a wet suit – as with all gear – do not settle for something that fails to fully meet your needs. Pick a suit based on fit and quality; you're likely to use it for a number of years and your comfort with it will affect the enjoyment of every dive you do in it. High price does not always equal high quality. Some suits are expensive but have a history of problems with fit, bad seams, poor quality neoprene, or inaccurate sizing. Fully customized suits are available; a number of measurements are taken and the material is cut, sewn, and glued to fit the individual. Such suits are more expensive, but you know that the suit fits the way it is supposed to. The downside to a full custom suit is that if the diver's measurements change very much, the suit may become a poor fit or become impossible to wear at all. Stock suits normally fit a bit less well, but offer more room for individual variation. This allows for some of that middle age spread or the new you who recently decided to get into better shape.

Dry Suits

Photo courtesy of Edge-HOG

Dry suits are chosen by those divers who spend a lot of time in colder water. For some divers, when the water temperature gets below a certain level, a wet suit is simply no longer an option. Dives of long duration are another circumstance in which dry suits are considered by many to be mandatory. A dry suit is a suit that insulates the diver with a layer of air as opposed to one of water. Coupled with undergarments of varying thicknesses to suit the environment, dry suits offer the best thermal protection for a recreational diver in cold water. The dry suit has two valves: one is used to add air and the other to allow it to escape. This is necessary for equalizing the suit as the diver descends and ascends; failing to do this can result in squeezes that can leave welts on a diver or create uncontrolled ascents. Dry suits have latex seals around the wrists, and latex or neoprene seals around the neck. The boots -- or in some cases, latex or neoprene socks – are attached to the legs. This makes a truly waterproof suit as long as there is no failure of a seal, zipper, or tear in the suit itself. The zipper on a dry suit, found on either the front or the back, is an extremely important component. Dry suit zippers are heavy and completely waterproof; the same type of zipper is used on suits worn by astronauts in outer space. Some suits have another zipper assembly over the main zipper to further protect it.

When choosing a dry suit, we first look at what material we want. Neoprene, crushed neoprene, vulcanized rubber, and what are known as shell suits are in use by divers around the world. Combinations of these materials are also used to maximize the suits' benefits.

Neoprene suits are warm and can be used with undergarments, but usually require the use of a significant amount of weight to offset the inherent buoyancy of the neoprene. They are very rugged though, and resist damage as well as remaining flexible.

Crushed neoprene is neoprene that has been compressed permanently to reduce the inherent buoyancy while still retaining much of the warmth and ruggedness of the material. Highly resistant to cuts and tears, the crushed suit is favored by many serious wreck divers.

Vulcanized rubber suits are not as warm as neoprene, but have one very distinct advantage -- they are easily decontaminated. Neoprene or shell suits can retain harmful chemicals present in the water. A vulcanized suit is the most popular choice when diving in waters that contain substances that must be cleaned off the diver.

Shell suits are perhaps the most popular style of dry suit used today. Made up of layers of different materials, they offer flexibility, resistance to damage, and cost effectiveness. Make no mistake – when compared to a wet suit, a dry suit is not cheap! The value comes from the range of temperatures in which dry suits can be used, the fact that they allow the diver a much longer (sometimes full year) dive season, and the lifespan of the suit. A wet suit can last the average diver three to five years based on 50-100 dives per year. A wet suit is well due for replacement when the neoprene begins to be permanently compressed and seams begin to come apart.

A properly maintained dry suit however, can last 15-20 years or more. Specific care is required: Seals need to be replaced, valves need to be serviced, and the zipper sometimes needs replacement if it has not been properly cared for. One of the drawbacks to a dry suit for a new diver is that it does require specific skills that a wet suit does not: inflating and deflating the suit while managing the BC, methods of correcting getting upside down and having the air in the suit rush to the feet, and choosing the proper undergarments. These issues require more effort of the new diver, but are manageable with proper instruction.

Semi-Dry Suits

Semi-dry suits are a combination of both wet and dry. A semi-dry suit is usually a neoprene suit that does not require an inflator. This is because the suit is filled with water and uses the same seals and zippers as a dry suit. Because of this layer of water, semi-dry suits are not subject to the compression that can occur with dry suits. What does happen though, is that the seals prevent the insulating layer of water from escaping at all. The result is that the amount of heat lost is much less than that from a wet suit and the diver stays warmer. While not as warm as a dry suit, the semi-dry suit can be an economical alternative to it.

Now that we have looked at the different types of suits, we can make some observations. Divers have many choices when it comes to exposure protection. The needs of every diver are different and must be considered when making such decisions. No one type or style will work for every diver. There are good choices, better choices, and best choices. Making those choices requires research, experience, and guidance from more experienced divers. We can safely say that when choosing a suit, cost is only one factor. Divers need to look at quality of construction, reputation of the manufacturer, and type of suit. Fit is critical with a suit; make sure that the suit that you buy is one that fits you the way it's supposed to. A wet suit should fit snugly, while a dry suit needs to allow the diver room to add air and undergarments along with allowing mobility. Both need to do this to keep the diver warm and as a result, safe. Following an exposure suit, a diver may choose to purchase a BC and/or regulator.

Buoyancy Compensators (BCs)

Photos courtesy of Edge-HOG

The BC is a crucial piece of dive gear, allowing us to control our position in the water column. It not only allows us to control our position, it also holds the tank. BCs come in two different basic configurations. The jacket style generally has a bladder that wraps around the diver as it inflates; the back inflate, as the name implies, has the bladder entirely on the back. The jacket style is perhaps most commonly used by new divers; it tends to keep divers more upright and higher in the water when on the surface. Let's look now at the basic component parts of a BC.

The BC needs an air cell to inflate and deflate, and it needs a way to accomplish that, which is done via the power inflator. A BC power inflator is a device that is connected to the bladder by a corrugated hose. This hose is generally located on the left side and connects to the BC in the area of the shoulder, though some are connected in the center of the air cell. The power inflator is also connected to the tank by the regulator's low pressure inflator hose. By pressing a button, air is allowed to flow into the BC. Another button is used to control a valve that allows air to escape the BC. When venting (allowing the air to escape) the BC, the inflator needs to be raised above the level of the connection to the BC or a trap – similar to that under your sink – is formed and the air cannot escape. Many BCs however, also have additional valves known as dump valves to allow air to be vented without using the power inflator. We all know that air will rise to the highest point underwater. When using the power inflator to vent, some models require the diver

117

to get nearly vertical in the water. Now, as we have previously discussed, divers do not swim vertically. Our ideal position is horizontal. Dump valves are often located on the right shoulder and the bottom of the BC on either side, allowing the diver to vent air without getting vertical. They can be used to release air very quickly or just a tiny bit at a time, providing the diver with whatever degree of control is required.

BCs may have pockets, D rings, pouches to contain weights, and numerous buckles to hold things together. There are some BCs that have very little beyond a few D rings; these are known as minimalist or basic harness type BCs. Commonly referred to as "back plate and wing" BCs, they are fully customizable in size, features, and function and also tend to cost much less than other BCs. They consist of a stainless steel, aluminum, or kydex plate, a simple one piece harness made of two inch nylon webbing, and a bladder (the wing) that is removable from the setup. Wings are available in different lifts to suit the type of dives, cylinder or cylinders used, and the amount of weight the diver requires. They commonly have three or four D rings, a buckle, and little or no extra padding, yet are very comfortable in the water. While not the most commonly used BCs, the great advantage of back plate and wing designs is that they can be set up to create a near perfect fit for any diver. Some believe that back inflate BCs tend to push a diver forward in the water. This is a myth. Back mounted BCs on a properly weighted diver do *not* push a diver face forward into the water.

Jacket style BCs are more commonly used and often have many "extras," but this does not mean they are the best choice for every diver. In my experience, these extras often add to the cost of the BC with little actual benefit to the diver. Pockets often seem to be poorly designed and inconveniently placed. Pockets that you can glue to the thighs of your exposure suit are much handier. There are often more D rings than the three or four found useful by most divers, or on some models, none at all.

How then do we choose a BC? The priorities must be comfort, quality, and features specific to the needs and preferences of the individual diver. Price is not a reliable barometer of any of these, and paying more does not guarantee you a "better" BC.

118

What matters is what the BC will do for you and how it will suit your needs. Always put this first in your decision to buy. What I look for in a BC is function. Whether one chooses a jacket style, back inflate, hybrid, or modular system like a back plate and wing, simple is better. Why? Because unnecessary complexity creates a more confusing piece of equipment, as well as creating too many potential failure points. It also involves unnecessary expense. There is simply no need for a diver to spend more than a few hundred dollars on a BC. For example, the last one I purchased was for a friend who then bought it from me. It was a used BC when I got it, and in excellent shape. The total cost was $75.00. It is not weight integrated, only has a couple D rings, and is a basic working BC. The pockets on it are actually well designed and usable. It is not what I would take on a 150 foot dive to a wreck in the Great Lakes, but its new owner has no intention of using it that way. For a warm-water diver who will not be using a dry suit or double cylinders, it is a great BC. It will serve its owner for many years doing the types of dives she does, and that is the ultimate goal in selecting a BC or any other piece of gear, for that matter.

Beware of claims that exotic BC features will make you a better diver. The only thing that will make you a better diver is good training and regular practice. I can take any BC that I can get on – regardless of size, style, or configuration -- and get horizontal and have full control over my buoyancy within ten minutes. This is the result of practice, experience, understanding the effects water has on me and my equipment, and proper weighting and trim. None of this is beyond the grasp of the average OW diver who wants to achieve this level of competence. A BC is a tool, and as with any tool, simple is usually better. The next items we'll look at are regulators.

Regulators

The item that allows us to breathe underwater was invented many years ago in a number of different forms. Regulators were used in industrial applications long before their relatively recent adaptation for underwater use in SCUBA diving. The modern SCUBA regulator is commonly attributed to two

Frenchmen, Emile Gagnan and Jacques Cousteau. In the 1940s, they began to work on a design that allowed a diver to descend underwater and be supplied air at ambient pressure (i.e., as the water pressure increased, the amount of air the regulator delivered also increased). This kept the pressure of the water from collapsing the diver's chest cavity -- a very good thing indeed. It also opened SCUBA diving to the average person. In the early days of diving, regulators (and most SCUBA gear) were sold in sporting goods stores and through mail order. I can even remember such equipment being in the Sears and Roebuck catalog. Dive shops were rare and training was done by ex-military divers, or one bought a book, ordered the gear, got air from somewhere, and went diving. Things are arguably much better now. The first regulators sold in the US by Gagnan and Cousteau were imported and sold at a sporting goods store in California. They were so popular that if you believe the accounts of everyone who claims to have bought one, you will note that more were purchased than were ever actually brought in.

Those early regulators were of the double hose design made famous by shows such as Sea Hunt. They worked well and were the most common type in use until the development of the single hose type we know today, which came into regular use in the 1950s. The single hose regulator is commonly divided into two basic types: the piston and the diaphragm. Each of them has subtypes known as balanced and unbalanced. The balanced regulator basically delivers air at the same rate, regardless of the pressure in the tank. Unbalanced regulators tend to get stiffer or breather harder as the tank pressure drops. What concerns us here is which kind of regulator we really need, and why.

A complete regulator set consists of several parts: the first stage, second stage (there are commonly two of them, a primary and an alternate or octo), the submersible pressure gauge (SPG) which may be in a console with other instruments such as a compass and depth gauge, and a low pressure (LP) inflator hose. Each of these plays a vital role in breathing underwater. We'll look at each of them in turn and then offer some advice on choosing a set.

The function of the first stage is to reduce the high air pressure in the tank to what is known as an intermediate pressure, and distribute it to the other components in the regulator set. This intermediate pressure varies from regulator to regulator, but is usually in the 135-145 psi range. This is the pressure that is sent to each second stage and the LP inflator hose. The SPG receives the full pressure in the tank, though it is restricted by a much smaller diameter orifice in the first stage and at the gauge itself. The hoses to each component that receive the intermediate pressure are of the same type and have the same size fitting at the first stage. The high pressure (HP) hose to the SPG usually has a larger diameter fitting. This is purposely done to avoid putting a low pressure hose on the high pressure side that would result in a rather spectacular failure of the hose and possible injury to those nearby. Early regulators did not have different size fittings and they may still be out there, so be careful when buying a used, older unit. The second stage on many regulators is a demand lever type. The user inhales or pushes the purge button and the diaphragm collapses onto the lever, allowing air to enter the chamber and be inhaled. The first stage responds to depth and pressure, and by way of the demand valve in the second stage, delivers a proper volume of air as depth increases or decreases. Many second stages have adjustment knobs that will allow you to fine-tune the amount of air you receive and/or vary the inhalation effort required to depress the lever. While a very nice and convenient feature, this adjustment is not absolutely necessary for the average recreational diver to have. It adds to the cost of the unit and for the casual diver, makes no real difference over a well-tuned, nonadjustable one.

The primary second stage (the one in the diver's mouth) often has an adjustment knob and a lever known as a venturi lever that is open or closed. Open, the venturi lever allows air to flow unobstructed to the diver. Closed, it deflects some of that air back up against the diaphragm, making it harder to depress. Why would we want this to happen? On the surface, a regulator that is finely tuned or adjusted to give the minimum amount of resistance to breathing will often free-flow if the purge is bumped or if the second stage is dropped upside down in water. The venturi lever prevents this from happening. It can also be used to stop a free-flow in combination with putting a thumb over the mouthpiece opening. The venturi lever, like the adjustment knob, is a nice feature but not strictly necessary.

The LP inflator hose has a quick-disconnect fitting that attaches to the LP inflator on the BC; it allows the diver to add air to the BC. There may be a second LP hose if a diver is using a dry suit. When not using a dry suit, a second LP hose may still be on the regulator and actually come in handy for something like a blowgun (for inflating lift bags) or for an emergency air horn. With some exceptions, these are standard connections. Non-standard connections are used on BCs that have a different type of inflator known as an integrated alternate, integrated octopus (octo), or integrated safe second. These inflator mechanisms combine a secondary breathing regulator with the power inflator. Hoses on these regulators have fittings that will only fit these mechanisms. The integrated octo is the subject of much debate. It does eliminate a hose from the regulator, which theoretically improves streamlining. It is also said to be easy to locate at the end of the power inflator. However, it also requires the donor in a low or out-of-air situation to donate the primary. There is nothing wrong with that for those who have been well trained in donating in that manner.

The problem is that few new divers are trained that way. They have been taught using standard setups that have a separate octo. If you choose a BC with a non-standard inflator as described above, it is completely reasonable to ask the shop to provide *instruction in the water* on its use. If they refuse, walk away. Do not attempt to use or purchase one of these units without instruction. You must control your buoyancy while donating, and for one trained on a standard setup this means venting while ascending. To vent with one of these units while breathing from the secondary, you'll have to remove it from your mouth repeatedly or use the shoulder dump on the opposite side (if the BC has one). *This is not something you want to do in a stressful situation without being completely comfortable in doing so.* Buddy breathing is the only way around this if there is no shoulder dump; this meets the need but is not even taught by many agencies today. This why I do not recommend these units to my students and I will not permit them in my Advanced Open Water class without seeing the diver use it. There are some class exercises in which this type of unit cannot physically be used at all. Another issue with these BCs is that if you decide to travel with one, it is advisable to also take a spare hose for the integrated alternate because if that hose fails, it may be difficult to find a replacement at your travel destination. It is advisable in any case to have a spare standard inflator hose for the regulator normally used with the BC equipped with this unit. If you own a BC like this and find yourself unable to use it for some reason, you can still use your regulator with a BC equipped with a standard inflator. If this is the case, you will still need to have a standard octo that you can put on the regulator or be fully familiar with buddy breathing, as you are no longer able to use the integrated second stage that is still attached to your own BC. I personally see too many unnecessary issues that can develop with the use of the integrated octo to make it a viable alternative.

While no part of the regulator is more important than another -- they are all vital -- the Submersible Pressure Gauge (SPG) is the most important gauge one can have. It tells you how much air is in your tank. In the early days of SCUBA, divers did not use them; they had another mechanism that indicated when they were running low on air. Called a "J" valve, it had a lever that functioned as a reserve supply. In the up position, this lever gave the diver roughly 300 psi of air that could be used for the ascent. The issue with these valves was that if the lever got hit or accidentally tripped, the diver might not know it. When the regulators began to breathe harder – indicating the air supply was getting low – the diver would reach back and pull down on the steel rod connected to the lever on the valve. With the valve already tripped, the diver had no reserve and had to make what could be too rapid an ascent to the surface, or hope a buddy was close enough to donate for a safe ascent. The SPG was a major step in resolving this issue.

The SPG is a simple device; it measures the pressure in the tank and indicates the reading on a dial, in most cases. While there are digital gauges available, including ones integrated into the dive computer, they offer no additional benefit but do add an additional potential failure point, as they are dependent on batteries. SPGs often indicate pressures up to 5000 psi, and 4000 psi gauges are common. They are relatively maintenance-free other than rinsing, and changing the O-rings in the connection to the hose. SPGs can be inaccurate by as much as 100-200 psi, which is another good reason to always keep at least 300-500 psi in the tank. As with any mechanical device they can fail, especially if water accidentally gets into them via the first stage and is not removed before the regulator is re-pressurized. In such a case, the gauge can be destroyed and the diver put at great risk. Anytime an SPG begins to act strangely, it should be replaced. If it does not read zero with the air off and no pressure in the system, does read zero when the tank is on, or seems to be way off in its readings when compared with a known gauge or pressure, throw it away and replace it. Gauges can be had for $40 to $80, depending on quality. Spend the money. Your life is worth much more than that.

We've now looked at the essential parts of the modern SCUBA regulator and have briefly described their functions. If you want to buy a regulator, what should you look for? First of all, how much do you realistically have to spend? A very good warm-water regulator can be had complete for around $400, including one with an adjustable second stage. Do you want a

124

piston or diaphragm? For the average recreational diver, it really makes no difference no matter what the shop may tell you. Balanced or unbalanced? This one can make a difference. A balanced unit will deliver the same volume of air with the same effort no matter what the depth may be or how low the tank gets. This is important in my opinion, as it eliminates one potential cause of diver stress (i.e., variable breathing effort). Anything that does that is good, so a balanced one it is.

The next consideration is the water temperature where you expect to dive. For warm-water diving (defined as above 40 degrees Fahrenheit, for most regulators), it makes no real difference. In colder or cold water, it does. Some regulators are not designed to be used in cold water and should not be, due to freeze-ups. Diaphragm regulators tend to be more resistant to this, so if it's the Great Lakes or deep inland quarries, a diaphragm makes the most sense. Another factor to consider is water quality. Some regulators are known as environmentally sealed, in that no water or other contaminants get into the first stage at all. Some allow water into parts of the first stage. No special unit is required for diving in warm, fresh water that is relatively clean, or for saltwater when the unit will always be carefully rinsed. If there is a lot of sediment in the water or other gunk that could cause a problem, a sealed regulator is called for, whether piston or diaphragm. For the strictly warm-water diver who takes good care of gear, most any first stage will be more than adequate. For anything else, I'd personally only choose an environmentally sealed first stage of the diaphragm type.

Now, what second stages should we consider? The temperature of the water continues to have some influence here. For cold water, I like the adjustable second stage that helps to regulate the amount of air I can get at one time. It reduces the chance of a free-flow due to the first stage freezing as a result of too much air being delivered. In warm water, I use both adjustable and non-adjustable second stages. One feature I also look for in a second stage is whether I can disassemble the stage underwater to clear it of anything that might get inside it. All of my personal regulators enable me to do this. I have seen dirt, twigs, and other debris get into a regulator; being able to fix that without surfacing is convenient. I just switch to my octo, remove the front cover, clear the obstruction, and put it back together. The next item to consider is the mouthpiece. There are many choices and no diver should have to deal with an uncomfortable one. There are even custom mouthpieces that can be molded to your own mouth. The mouthpiece should be comfortable enough to allow you to do a dive of any length with no jaw pain or fatigue.

It might seem prudent to save a few dollars by buying an alternate second stage (octo) that is cheaper than the primary. After all, it will hardly ever be used. However, when it *is* used it will be during a high stress situation (you are donating to an out-of-air diver) and that is not the time to be dealing with inferior equipment. The octo should be of equal quality to the primary. You should be able to adjust or detune it enough to prevent it from free-flowing and still deliver an adequate volume of air. If you service your own regulator and have the same model for both second stages, you can keep just one type of kit on hand instead of two different ones. Again, I recommend that divers choose a standard octo over the integrated type. There is less maintenance involved, they are most likely what you were trained with, and they usually cost less than the integrated type. Standard octos can also be used on most BCs you will ever rent or borrow. The brief summary on second stages is this: For warm water, any second stage of reasonable quality will do. For colder water, you should get an adjustable second that can be disassembled under water. Match either with a standard octo of equal quality.

The LP hose is a simple matter of finding one that is the right length for the BC you are using. It should also have the correct connector for the LP inflator. Remember that if the hose has been used on a BC with an integrated inflator, it will most likely not work on a standard BC. There is an adaptor available, but it adds to the length of the hose and creates another failure point. A second LP hose can be added if you choose to get a dry suit. This will be connected to the inflator valve on the suit.

The high pressure hose and gauges are the final parts of the regulator that we need to consider. The most common configuration new divers are likely to see is the console setup.

The console will always include at least the SPG and a depth gauge or dive computer. There may also be a compass. Individual divers tend to have personal preferences as to the configuration, based on training and style of diving. I prefer wrist-mounted gauges, for example, but many do not. If you do plan on getting a console setup, make sure it is organized in the way that suits you best. If it has a compass, try to get a console that will allow you to see both the compass and the depth gauge at the same time. Some do not, and this makes it difficult to successfully navigate a course. When choosing a hose length, select one that allows you to easily lift the gauge to see it, without excess length to get in the way otherwise. For the average diver using a console, a 30-36 inch length is usually sufficient. If you decide to go with a wrist-mounted depth gauge and compass or computer, a simple SPG hose of approximately 24 inches will do quite nicely.

To sum up about regulators: For warm-water dives, any regulator (piston or diaphragm) by any major manufacturer will be completely satisfactory. There is no need for a warm-water diver to spend extra money for a cold-water regulator. An environmentally sealed first stage is always a good option, though. For cold-water divers, the best choice would be an environmentally sealed, diaphragm first stage, coupled with an adjustable second stage to lessen the chance of a free-flow. For both setups, I recommend a standard octo rather than an integrated one. Most new divers are trained with the standard setup and if you are partnered with a new buddy, it will reduce or eliminate any confusion in a low or out-of-air situation. Finally, if you're not going with wrist-mounted gauges, choose a console that will allow you to view the compass and depth gauge at the same time.

Dive Computers

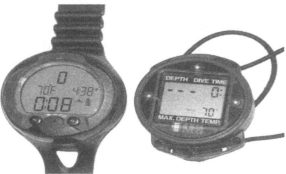

It would be impossible to describe every dive computer available in any real detail, but this section can serve as a general overview to get you started. Dive computers currently range from relatively inexpensive bottom timers to computers that have full color displays and can be programmed with up to ten gas mixes for technical divers. Some even have the ability to monitor the diver's heart rate. Some are worn on the arm, some are installed in consoles, and a few are built right into dive masks. Most allow the dive information to be downloaded into a home computer or laptop. All of them work using decompression algorithms developed for SCUBA diving. Many of these are the same algorithms used on standard dive tables; the difference is that computers keep much more accurate track of the dive.

While tables use the maximum depth of the dive (which assumes a square profile) to determine nitrogen loading, computers sample depth at regular intervals throughout the dive. Some allow the user to set the sampling rate: the more frequent the rate of sampling, the more accurate the profile of the dive. The square profile assumed by dive tables gives a generous margin of error. Most real dives have many variations such as a gradual descent and ascent along a slope, depth variations caused by natural features, and decisions made along the way by the diver. A computer tracks these variations in enough detail to result in more time being credited towards the No Decompression Limits. The diver is therefore able to stay down longer and *theoretically* still be safe.

Theoretically, because the algorithms used in these computers are not able to take the physiology of the individual into account. They also cannot factor in dehydration, a cold, or any other condition that may raise the risk of decompression sickness (DCS). For these reasons, choosing a computer is a big decision. In addition to cost, you must factor in your needs, interests, and level of discipline. The last is one of the biggest downfalls I have seen to computer use among new divers and why I do not recommend them for new divers; this will be addressed in more detail at the end of this section. For those who have the discipline to use the computer as a backup to the brain, I can make a few recommendations. The first factor to consider is what type of dives you plan to do and whether you will need a computer with Nitrox capability. If not, a number of basic computers are available that are set to determine nitrogen loading using only 21% air. These relatively inexpensive computers will serve the average diver well for years.

For those who do wish to use Nitrox, the number of computers out there is varied, ranging in price from nicely affordable to ridiculously expensive. Available in wrist or console, these computers are of greatest benefit to the diver who will be using different gas mixes. The average recreational diver with a Nitrox certification will typically use mixes from 22% up to 40%. Nitrox computers will allow you to change the mix, though some computers will require you to wait a set amount of time to do so. This is done to prevent the accidental or intentional switching of gasses that could result in a dangerous situation. For example, if you were using 32% Nitrox with a maximum operating depth of 111 feet and accidentally switched the computer to calculate for air, the computer could not alert you to a problem if you descended below that depth. You would risk taking a central nervous system (CNS) hit from too high an oxygen partial pressure level. The computer should only be used as backup for the brain. The dive computer *does not relieve you of the responsibility* to calculate the Maximum Operating Depth for the gas used, keep track of the partial pressures, and monitor your own CNS clock. Some training is making tables and manual calculations optional, or even eliminating them. The safest divers will make it their business to know how these calculations work anyway, because computers can fail. Divers who know what their computer should say, and why, will recognize a computer problem immediately. Divers who depend on their computers with no real comprehension of what the readings mean may not; those divers are at higher risk.

Presuming you have decided to buy a computer and are committed to using it appropriately, which one is best for you, the new diver? Quite simply, the one that will do what you ask of it, in a manner that is clear and easy to understand. Look for a computer that does not require you to go through numerous steps to use its basic functions. There are now online classes for many models. Other users will often take time to tutor new owners through message boards, e-mail, and in person. The dive shop where you purchase your computer should, at a minimum, offer free basic instruction in the use of the models they sell. If they do not, look for another shop or ask that they either cover the cost or offer a coupon from the manufacturer for the online course. The reason for this is that like any other electronic device today, the manual that comes with many computers is thick, jammed with small print, and often poorly written. The shocking part is that the manufacturers know this but have elected not to address it, so it is up to the user to figure out how to use the new device. Many do this by simply trying to figure the computer out a bit on the surface, then diving with it, hoping they'll figure it out as they go. Unless you already have a bit of familiarity with computers, you are far better off making the effort to get adequate instruction.

Value is an important consideration when choosing a computer. Don't assume that one computer is better than another because it costs more, and don't think that a used computer sold by a trusted friend or shop is not as good as a new one. Consider the experienced diver who is moving into mixed gasses and needs to upgrade to a computer that will handle trimix; that diver's perfectly good basic air or Nitrox computer may now be for sale at a fraction of the cost of a new one.

Finally, choose a style of computer that will work the best for you. Some may like a console type while others prefer a wrist mount. Choose a display that you can read easily, and

130

remember that this will become more challenging as you get into middle age and beyond. Even though I have a mask with my bifocal prescription, I still prefer a computer with a large display. Consider whether you want a computer that can backlight the display; at night or on low visibility dives, this is a must. Most do, but make sure this is an option. Some may allow you to set the duration of the backlighting.

The computer ultimately chosen is not as important as how it is used. I'm not referring to the manufacturer's directions here, but rather the need to use any dive computer with common sense and safety in mind. The more simplified the average OW class becomes, the more important it is to remember that. I made mention earlier of discipline in using a computer. Many new computer owners trust the computer too much; I, myself, was guilty of this in the beginning of my diving career. The course I took taught tables but I was encouraged to buy a computer early on. I did not resist the idea. A computer you used underwater? Cool! It was sold to me as something that would extend my dive time and allow me to do more dives. Even cooler! It would keep track of my nitrogen and watch my ascent rate. I would not have to think as much, I could just enjoy being underwater. While I suffered no ill effects, it became clear to me as my diving progressed that I was taking more and more chances. I was diving deeper, for longer, and with less regard for the consequences. I allowed the computer to lull me into a false sense of security. When I started to delve into technical diving and went back to diving tables and planning my dives based on those, I found that I actually enjoyed the dives more. Planning dives myself put me more in touch with what was actually going on, and also gave me real sense of accomplishment. I now plan and track all dives using tables even though I still have the computer with me.

Other Accessories

An entire additional book could be devoted to the many accessories available to divers. Here, we'll just cover a few that I consider essential for the beginner, prioritized as always, based on how the diver's safety can be enhanced. First, a safety sausage of some type should be considered. I personally like the one in the Surface Signaling Kit from Divers Alert Network

(DAN). It is big (meaning it can be seen from greater distances) and comes with a mirror, whistle, and battery-powered light as additional signaling devices. It can be inflated orally, with a low pressure hose, or with an octo. It has an overpressure relief valve and can be deployed from depth with a reel or finger spool. It also has 40 lbs of lift and can be used as a lift bag or emergency flotation device. There are other, similar designs which are also very good, but the DAN sausage is my personal choice. Some tropical operators and even dive shops sell sausages that are nice and small for convenient carrying, but are made of such flimsy material that they are little more than long trash bags -- stay away from these! Spend the few extra dollars and get a true sausage that you can rely on.

The next item you can consider is some type of audible signaling device. Until the invention of the power air horn, the first device used by divers was a good whistle. Whistles are still a good choice and will work well in relatively calm conditions; higher wind will carry away their sound, rendering them much less effective. They are usually plastic, to resist the effects of saltwater, but should still be rinsed after every dive with the rest of your gear. If you can find a good lifeguard or police whistle made of stainless steel or with a good nickel plating, these are more expensive but more rugged. As with all gear, these metal whistles need to be rinsed and dried well after each dive to prevent corrosion. Some BCs come with a whistle attached, but these are usually not loud enough, in my opinion. They are often attached in inconvenient places and because they are so small, they could be easily lost. The power air horn is available in versions that work above water only, or both above and underwater. The dual purpose ones are not ones I'd choose as they generally have far less range than that of dedicated surface units. The original power air horn, the Dive Alert®, is reported to have a range of one mile over calm seas. Because this signal is so loud, it is recommended that you (and other divers with you) duck underwater before sounding it, in order to prevent ear damage. This kind of volume is a welcome comfort when you are in sight of the boat but no one is looking your way. Set this off and everyone will be looking for the source.

Dive lights are the next essential safety item to be considered. Even on daylight dives, a light is a valuable tool, illuminating dark crevices and also restoring full spectrum color. At 80 or 90 feet, everything looks greenish blue. Shine a good light on a part of the reef though, and watch as colors you could only dream of explode into life. Lights are mandatory on night dives and many deep dives; without them, you won't see anything. They are used for illuminating the area, picking out features, and for communication. At night or in very low visibility, light communication often takes the place of hand signals. Lights can also be used to illuminate a slate or wetnotes.

So, what do we look for in a dive light? First of all, it needs to be waterproof! This sounds obvious, but there are lights advertised as water resistant, which look like dive lights, but which are not actually meant to be used at depth. A dive light is normally rated to at least 300 feet; many are rated to 500 feet or more. The recreational diver has many choices, from small lights that work well on daytime reef dives while serving as backup lights for night dives, to high-powered lights used by cave and shipwreck divers. All are battery powered, using either standard batteries or rechargeable units. The lights used by cave and wreck divers are generally overkill for the average open water diver, but can be used that way if desired. Be aware though, that these lights start at around $500 and go up from there, while a very good recreational light can be had for as little as $20 to $30. Features to look for in a light include a rugged housing (thermoplastic material or machined aluminum), a focused beam, and a reliable switch. A dive light should be shock resistant, able to withstand pressure, and have double O-ring seals. These O-rings will need to be kept clean and *lightly* lubricated with silicone grease; if too much grease is used, it can trap sand or dirt, compromising the seal.

133

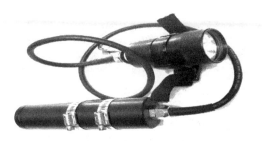

The beam on a dive light should be more focused than that of a standard flashlight. Underwater, light is rapidly dispersed by refraction and reflection off particles in the water. A dive light beam must be focused and intense enough to cut through the interference -- this measure of a light's performance is usually defined as its beam angle. A beam angle of about 10 degrees is desirable, but beams tighter than that can be very valuable for signaling. A wider beam can be used if it has a center hot spot, while too wide an angle will just disperse and not have a very effective range. Some of the more expensive lights have focusable beams and can be used in a variety of conditions.

The final feature to consider on any light is the switch. If a light is going to fail, generally it will fail when being turned on or off. If the switch is a mechanical one, its failure may also result in flooding of the light, because part of the switch penetrates the case. For this reason, lights without mechanical switches may be preferable. Look for lights with magnetic switches or which activate when the lens or part of the housing is rotated – they tend to be more reliable and less prone to failure. A recent development in dive light technology is the light emitting diode (LED), identifiable by its blue-white light that is more intense than that of a normal bulb. LEDs are at least as bright as conventional lights, use less power, offer longer burn times and are not nearly as fragile as bulbs, so may someday be standard in all lights.

Cutting Instruments

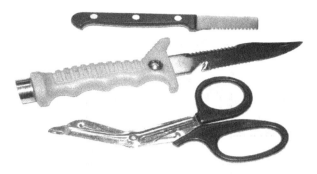

When we consider cutting instruments for underwater, we are generally talking about knives or shears. No matter which we choose – and many choose both – these tools should be resistant to corrosion. Stainless steel, titanium, ceramics, and even carbon fiber can now be forged or molded into cutting instruments that are not affected by fresh or saltwater. In the early days of exploration underwater, knives tended to be large Bowie type knives; they conveyed a macho image and made excellent pry bars but were not very useful for much else... unless it was to fight off the occasional shark or barracuda that everyone was warned about. We now realize that the true danger underwater comes more from us than from the life that exists in the sea. When we choose a cutting tool to take with us, we now consider different needs. There is more danger from monofilament fishing line, for example, than from sharks or barracudas. Even worse are drift nets and steel leaders used on ocean fishing lines. Let's look, then, at what is most useful for these hazards.

Knives for diving have evolved over the years. The huge pig-stickers of the past have been replaced by small, easily carried blades with blunt tips and partially serrated edges. These knives are designed for use on rope, nets, webbing, and fishing line; some have a small, razor-sharp notch specifically for line. Many tech divers now carry a small, serrated knife that looks like a steak knife with the point cut off and filed. Blunt tips are preferred as they are stronger, less likely to injure the diver, and less likely to damage a suit or other gear.

Tech divers will also carry a small knife known as a Z knife; it is a simple, replaceable utility knife blade in a holder that can slice through monofilament like a hot knife through butter. In addition, divers now carry shears similar to those carried by EMTs. Made of stainless steel and capable of cutting through a penny, they are cheap, easily replaceable, and reliable. They can also be used with heavy gloves, making them a favorite of cold-water divers. It is good practice to carry a backup for your knife, as it is to carry a backup light for night-diving. There is a saying among those of us who prescribe to Hogarthian diving (named after William Hogarth Main). It states that if an item is not needed, don't take it on the dive. If it is needed, take two!

Slates and Wetnotes

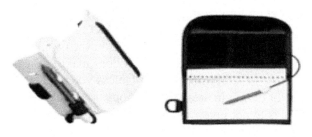

Slates and wetnotes are two items that I consider essential to good diver communication. The ability to actually put in writing what you wish to say eliminates the confusion that may result from hand signals. They are also very valuable for keeping track of course changes, important features, and logging sights you may wish to accurately document. These notes can be transferred to the actual dive log or used for reference when editing photos or videos. Slates are generally made of some type of plastic. Slates are available in a variety of sizes and with different options. Some come with an attached compass to aid in navigation. There are also slates that have multiple pages and are curved to be worn on the arm. Pencils used on them are no different than those used by golfers, though some are made of graphite with a plastic cover that is hardier in underwater use.

Wetnotes are actual notebooks made of waterproof paper. This paper is treated to withstand repeated submersion and works very well. It can be written on and even erased several times before it needs to be replaced. Wetnotes are very popular with technical divers for keeping alternate decompression stop information and communicating the sometimes detailed information technical divers require. For the recreational diver, they offer the benefit of being able to keep pages of information that would soon fill up a slate. I highly recommend them.

Cylinders (Tanks)

The final item we are going to look at is your cylinder, commonly called a tank. In light of the fact that few new divers purchase their own tanks immediately after the OW class, I am not going to go into great detail, but it does make sense to provide some general information. Unless you plan on doing a great deal of diving in areas where shops or air fills are limited, my advice is to not invest in tanks right away. They are the most common item rented to new divers and nearly every dive shop has a supply readily available. If you are going to travel to dive, nearly all resorts and dive boats include them in the price of diving.

It makes sense to have your own tanks when you are doing a lot of diving, to the point where owning begins to be cheaper than renting. Another reason to have your own is if you live in an area where renting tanks is not always convenient, or if there are often times when you just have to get wet, but can't get to the dive shop. Being able to go out to the garage, grab a couple tanks, load the car and head for the nearest waterhole is a nice option, but also one that many divers simply do not need. If you do elect to buy your own tanks, be sure that your diving justifies the added expense of owning them. In addition to the initial cost, you must consider the price of annual visual inspections, along with hydrostatic testing every five years if you live in the United States. Overseas readers may find that the testing is required more often.

Another factor to consider is space. Do you have room to store tanks in your home? I bought my first set of tanks while living in a small apartment. It was sometimes very inconvenient to have them sitting in the living room, kitchen, or bedroom. About the only place they did not make an appearance was the bathroom. It sounds funny, but really can be an annoyance if you start accumulating them. I now own over a dozen tanks of various sizes and during dive season, it is not uncommon to find a set of doubles leaning up against the cabinets in the kitchen. Living alone, this is not a big problem. If you live with a non-diver, it could become a serious issue the first time that person kicks or trips over one of them. There is also a great deal of misinformation and ignorance of SCUBA gear amongst the general public. While it is a fact that tanks are under high pressure and have a great deal of stored energy, they are not like those that contain flammable gasses. However, some apartment complexes and homeowners associations have filed complaints over divers storing tanks and have, in some cases, forbidden their presence. This is something to think about before you bring tanks home, at least in broad daylight where nosy neighbors can see them.

Finally, if you do decide to buy tanks after looking at all the reasons in a thoughtful manner, talk to your instructor, your mentor if you have one, and most importantly, other divers not connected with selling them to you. Research the types and sizes, decide on aluminum or steel, and use your rate of air consumption to decide on the size of tank that will best suit your diving. Compare prices and look for long-term value. Steel tanks are more expensive, but have longer service lives. Aluminum tanks may be half the price (or less) of steel tanks, but have shorter service lives. There is no one tank that is right for every diver, so the selection of yours should be based on your needs. What I would suggest for one diver would not be correct for another in similar conditions but with different gas needs. The best advice is to actually dive with different tanks and see what works best for you. Don't allow yourself to be talked into buying tanks based on price alone. Use the other lessons you have learned through this book to put together an analysis of your needs and do the homework necessary to make a smart and informed choice. It will be another example of taking responsibility for your own dives and dive planning.

General Considerations in Configuring Gear

When it comes to equipment, I ascribe to the following principles, adapted from the technical equipment recommendations of the International Association of Nitrox and Technical Divers (IANTD) program. The following should be true for all equipment used by the recreational diver:

1. Safe and reliable.

2. Comfortable and well-fitting.

3. Provide for adequate redundancy without being excessive.

4. Configured for self-sufficiency and self-rescue.

5. Simple and streamlined.

6. All accessories are easily reachable.

7. Allow for buddy assist and rescue.

8. Has a low-drag profile (streamlined).

9. Adaptable to the diver's needs.

10. Adaptable to the diver's objectives.

11. All equipment identifiable by touch and location.

12. Standardized with fellow divers yet versatile to meet the needs of the user.

13. Equipment placement is balanced and instinctive.

14. Any changes have been made gradually and with careful thought.

15. Diver is open to improvement to his or her setup.

16. All cylinders are properly labeled with the gas mixture, MOD, and the diver's name.

We'll look at each of these principles in more detail now, along with some options divers have for following them.

1. When we speak of safe and reliable equipment, divers can be assured of this when dealing with products from virtually any manufacturer of SCUBA equipment today. The problem usually comes from equipment that is not regularly and professionally maintained, not kept clean and rinsed, or is not suitable for the environment.

2. Comfortable and well-fitting gear is essential to every diver. Problem gear can introduce unwanted task loading, which can increase diver stress and risk. Proper exposure protection is essential.

3. Providing for adequate redundancy without being excessive is a key component of technical diving, but is also a principle that is useful for the new diver. This is why most divers take a kit of spare parts when they travel to a dive site, and why you should always have a backup light with you on a night dive.

4. When we talk about gear configured for self-sufficiency and self-rescue, we are not talking about configuring the equipment for solo diving. We mean equipment that allows the diver to make use of every feature in the event of a buddy separation or when it is a relatively simple matter to address a problem on one's own. Overly-complicated configurations add to task loading and increase the risk in the event of a problem. While the purpose of diving with a buddy is to look out for each other and reduce risk, you should be capable of rescuing yourself in the event of an emergency.

5. Simple and streamlined gear is a common sense principle that only adds to the safety of the team. Complicated gear with many "bells and whistles" just introduces additional task loading and more potential failure points. Streamlined gear reduces swimming effort and air consumption. Streamlining is taught or at least mentioned in every Basic Open Water class, but

you would not know it by looking at some of the OW divers on boats around the world!

6. All accessories being easily reachable is another common sense item. Any item carried on a dive should be easily accessible by the diver, preferably with either hand. All items should also be easily accessible to the diver's buddy. Carrying an item that is to be used on the dive and having to go through complicated maneuvers to reach it can result in delayed reaction times and increased stress.

7. Gear must allow for buddy assist and rescue. This is an extension of the pre-dive buddy check, but it goes a bit further. Not only should buddies be familiar with each other's gear, but the gear should be configured so that in the event of an incident, the buddy can easily remove or adjust the gear to aid the victim. Any gear changes should be made with this principle in mind; make sure that it is always easy for others to assist you if you need it.

8. Gear should have a low drag profile for several reasons, the main one being to reduce swimming effort. The lower physical exertion reduces one risk factor for decompression sickness (DCS) while also reducing air consumption, increasing the diver's general level of comfort, and reducing the diver's overall stress. Clean, simple, streamlined divers serve as good role models for others, and earn the respect of boat captains, mates, and Divemasters that see a diver who is skilled, competent, and safe.

9. Equipment must be adaptable to the diver's needs. This means that as the diver gains experience or changes the type of diving done, gear can be updated as needed without fundamentally changing the base equipment. Certain types of equipment configurations (like basic harness BCs) lend themselves to this more easily than others. Seek out a dive professional or mentor who can help you determine the gear

configuration that will give you the best adaptability within your means and needs.

10. Gear that is adaptable to the diver's objective is a principle specific to those who expect to dive in a variety of markedly different conditions. For those divers, gear must be usable with a variety of exposure suits, in warm water or cold, fresh water or salt, and be easy to take on trips. Some divers don't mind owning several sets of gear to cover all contingencies, but for those who do, this principle is key. It is a good principle for any diver to keep in mind when choosing gear, in case of unanticipated future changes.

11. All equipment should be identifiable by touch and location. Making sure that you know where every piece of equipment is by touch assures that no matter what the dive conditions are, accessing an item is instinctual, smooth, and quick. This reduces task loading and diver stress. It helps to place your accessories in the same places for every dive. For example, if you carry EMT shears and place them in the same BC pocket every time you dive, you'll instantly know where to reach when you find yourself dealing with some monofilament line. Wasting time and energy searching multiple locations for your shears would increase your stress level and possibly, the severity of your entanglement problem. This could lead to panic, and panic tends to kill divers.

12. Equipment should be standardized with fellow divers yet versatile to meet the needs of the user. If someone needs to assist you, you want them to be able to easily identify and operate key elements of your gear; the easiest way to accomplish this is for you and those you dive with to configure gear in a similar manner. Valuable time will then be saved in any stressful or emergency situation you may eventually encounter. At the same time, it is your gear and needs to serve your needs very specifically and efficiently to enhance your diving experience and general safety. It is up to you to configure gear in a manner which best

meets your personal requirements while making it easy to assist you if the need arises.

13. Equipment placement is balanced and instinctive. Balanced means all equipment is placed in a manner that enhances trim, because poor trim increases diver effort and stress. Instinctive placement means that the equipment is located where it makes sense for it to be, is easy for the diver to find, and easy for a buddy to find when assistance is needed. Moments wasted unnecessarily looking for or fiddling with gear are sometimes moments that affect diver safety.

14. Any equipment changes have been made gradually and with careful thought. When you add or subtract an item or change a part of your equipment, you should carefully consider the consequences of doing so. You should first ask yourself if it will affect your safety. Will it add to your task loading? Is it necessary for you to make the change? What benefit will you get from making it? Make changes only when necessary and then introduce change in small steps, giving yourself time and practice to adapt to one new thing before introducing the next. Don't make changes on a whim, because someone you know has a similar setup, or because the local dive shop said it was the latest, best thing. Even the latest, best thing can turn out to be junk for the diver who does not truly need it.

15. Divers should always be open to improving their setups. Even after you think you've chosen the perfect equipment for yourself, there may come a time when more experienced divers point out potential improvements. Such input should be considered thoughtfully, neither mindlessly accepted because it comes from someone you assume knows better, nor reflexively rejected because you've already made your own decisions. If you can see the sense of the suggestion, its benefit to you, and feel able to implement it, you should at least be open to the idea.

16. All cylinders are properly labeled with the gas mixture, maximum operating depth (MOD), and the diver's name. This idea comes from technical diving, and is relevant for those who dive with Nitrox, also known as Enriched Air. Many think the correct way to label Nitrox tanks is with a label the size of a bumper sticker. Large labels involve unnecessary cost, can disguise defects in a tank, may promote rusting on steel tanks, and must be replaced with every visual inspection. A simpler system is this: Tanks carry an "O2 clean" sticker once they've been cleaned for use with Nitrox. Just add to this a piece of duct tape with the gas mixture (as tested by the diver), the MOD, the diver's name, and the date of the gas analysis. This way, all the necessary information is easily available and there's no significant labeling cost to the diver when changing gas mixes. Some use tags on the valve with this information; I do not recommend these as they can get caught on things (interfering with handling of the tank) or get separated from the tank completely.

What You Should Know Before You Buy

I prefer that students have the option to try gear in a pool and find items that fit and work for them before investing their money in it. To make students buy gear that they have not had the opportunity to try is somewhat shortsighted. You can't know if the gear you have is right for you until you have actually used it in the water. Some shops have liberal return policies, others do not. Before you buy any piece of equipment, make sure that you know exactly what is required for the class. Before spending any money, ask for the opportunity to try the items you might wish to buy. If the dealer believes in the gear that much, it should not be a problem. They should have demo items available for just this purpose; if they do not, ask them why they don't. Ask them for the names of other students who have purchased the same items. Lastly, get on the Internet and research the items, compare prices, read reviews, and ask questions on message boards. Tell the shop you want to do this. If the items they are selling you are good and priced fairly, they should have no problem with this.

If a shop objects, it may be out of fear that you will buy the items online at a cheaper price. The fact is that you may indeed find gear for what appears to be less expense. You also need to consider shipping costs and most importantly, service after the sale (from both the online retailer and from the shop providing your certification courses). Some shops may not allow you to use gear you bought elsewhere, or they may treat you with less than stellar attitudes. To some degree this is understandable; they do have to make a living. One way to avoid this altogether is to get instruction from an independent instructor. They usually do not sell gear and have a much better attitude towards students buying gear from wherever they get the best deals.

The downside is that buying gear online may not have the return option and you will not be able to try on several different items before you buy. There is always the possibility that given a chance, your local shop may match or at least come close to the Internet retailer's prices. A little known truth about the SCUBA equipment industry is that there is often a large markup on gear (up to 200% or more, depending on the item). Retailers often have a great deal of room to negotiate.

Some items do not have big markups because of manufacturer policies concerning minimum prices. MSRP, MARP, MAP and MSP are all terms used in the SCUBA industry. The Manufacturers Suggested Retail Price (MSRP) is familiar to most, but the others may not be.

The Minimum Advertised Retail Price (MARP) is set by some manufacturers and is the price below which retailers may not go when advertising items for retail sale. Illegal in some areas, it is in wide use by the SCUBA industry. It is used to keep dealers from truly competing with each other. It is agreed by the dealer when he takes on the line of gear that he will not advertise those items in "sales promotions" that would give him an "unfair advantage" over other dealers of the same item. Next time you see a sale on gear from an authorized dealer, go online or call around and see if it truly is a sale limited to that one retailer. Most times it is not, unless it is a discontinued, outdated, or overstocked item on which the dealer has gotten permission to advertise a lower price. The MARP does not prevent the retailer from *selling* the item at a lower price even

146

than advertised, though that lower price may be limited by the manufacturer. This means the dealer may have some room to move on the final transaction price if the advertised price is too high for you; it never hurts to try negotiating for more of a discount.

The Minimum Advertised Price (MAP) is the lowest price a dealer may use in advertisements for any reason, including special sales and promotions. Unlike the MARP, it does not prevent him from actually advertising the item at lower than the regular retail price, as long as he has first received permission from the manufacturer to do so. If he advertises a lower price without prior permission, he could face sanctions from the manufacturer, up to having his dealer agreement terminated. This is why you may see an item advertised at a price and described as being on sale, and if you were to check around you would see that it *is* different than what other retailers are asking. That could be due to the item being from one of the previously described categories (discontinued, outdated, or overstock) that the manufacturer needs to move. Again, the dealer may actually be permitted to sell at a lower price, but may not be advertising the full savings that are possible. Ask if there are any discounts available.

The Minimum Selling Price (MSP) is used by a couple manufacturers of what some consider high-end gear. This equipment cannot be sold to the consumer at less than the stated price for any reason without the express permission of the manufacturer. If a dealer does sell something below this price and it is discovered, it is possible that their dealer status will be terminated. Usually when a complaint is filed, it is by another dealer who is honoring the MSP (and therefore lost the sale to the dealer who violated the agreement). It is fairly easy to determine who these manufacturers are -- just go on any Internet message board and ask. Because these restrictive trade practices are illegal in Europe, a "grey market" has emerged for these same lines. The gear is purchased in large quantities at a discount by European dealers, who then resell the gear to American dealers who offer it below the MSP. The manufacturer will not warranty these purchases even though it is the exact same gear. They do this – supposedly – to protect

147

their dealers. They claim that these sales are not authorized, while making the discounted supply available outside the US.

So what does all this mean to the average diver? Quite a bit, in fact. When you decide to purchase gear, you have many choices. Price is only one factor and one that should never truly dictate your purchase. Price does not necessarily track with higher quality or lower quality. A name does not guarantee that a piece of equipment is better or worse than a similar item. There are divers and various gear vendors who will tell you unequivocally that what they carry, use, or recommend is the absolute best. The fact is, this is not true. You may hear outrageous claims about one brand over another. If a dealer tells you Brand X is junk and you risk your life using it, this may be an honest professional expressing a genuine concern, or it could be someone trying to make a sale that will help the shop more than it will help you. Do some research and find out for yourself. Look for brands that allow the dealer to decide what they want to charge you. Look for brands that will meet your needs and not force you to go beyond your financial means. Consider buying used gear for some items; fins, for example, really do not wear out. Other items that can be bought used at great savings are regulators, BCs, computers, and even exposure suits, *if you know what to look for*.

Does Renting Gear Make Sense for You?

I hope this chapter has opened your eyes to the choices you have when it comes to equipment, and given you strategies for making those choices wisely. You do not have to spend a fortune to get good quality gear, and shouldn't allow yourself to be talked into buying something you don't need or can't afford. When it comes to equipment, take your time. Talk to more experienced divers and dive professionals to educate yourself as well as possible, then choose based on your needs and means. Anyone who pressures you to buy a certain item is showing disrespect for your ability to make your own decisions; they may be speaking from personal bias or interest rather than trying to help you find what works best for you. As with diving in general, you are responsible for your own safety and that includes what gear you buy. Take the time to do your

148

homework before you choose, and your choices will be good ones.

Once you have done this, the next question you will have to answer is whether you buy your own gear or rent, or buy some gear and rent the rest. There are advantages and disadvantages to each option. Many factors will have a bearing on your decision: the type of diving you do, the diving you plan to do, how often you dive, what you can afford, the amount of storage space you have, your willingness to keep up with necessary gear maintenance, and whether you find the convenience of renting worth the trade-offs it entails.

Making this decision should involve the same careful thought you devote to any other aspect of diving. New divers generally invest in a basic kit of mask, snorkel, fins, and boots, and perhaps an exposure suit. Due to the importance of comfort and fit, these are all good choices. If you plan to go any further than this, be careful. Some new divers are encouraged to buy additional gear right away. I was one of those who purchased a large amount of gear very early. In fact, I took my OW class in all of my own equipment, including tanks. While I don't regret doing this, I look back now and see that there were times when waiting and renting certain items would have been beneficial. As my diving progressed, my needs changed and within two years, I had replaced or modified every item except my prescription mask. Interests, needs, and wants all changed direction from my original plan. A great deal of money was spent in a short amount of time. I could have spent much less, had I taken just a bit of time to try different things. On the other hand, I was doing a lot of diving; nearly every other weekend was spent in the water. It was convenient for me to not be dependent on what equipment was available for rental at a given time, and I had no worries about getting stuck with unfamiliar gear.

The dive shop I was using at the time had a weekend gear-rental rate of $75 for students. It would have cost $150 per month to dive. At the time, I was also working a great deal of overtime and had money to spend. And everything looked so cool. Not the best reason to make a major purchase of equipment. As I write this, there is enough gear in my office to equip four divers plus some extras. As an instructor this is almost a necessity, but for the recreational diver it is serious overkill. One set of gear is all most divers will really need, and that is only if they dive regularly.

For the once-a-year or occasional diver who also dives locally, owning equipment is not necessarily the best option. When you look at rental costs versus the cost of owning, renting may well be the most economical option for occasional diving. This assumes you can rent gear that is in good shape, available when you need it, and not overpriced. It's a definite bonus if the shop has various types of equipment available. Had I been able to try different styles of BC and regulator combinations, I would likely have saved some money by buying once instead of twice. I do know that I still would have bought my own gear. I am a big proponent of diving locally and diving as often as possible. Not having the time or means to travel extensively, I need to dive locally to stay sharp and just to get underwater. The reality of this is that many local diving options do not have shops on site, let alone rental gear. Having my own gear means I can pick up anytime, load the car, drive to the site, and dive. No need to see if the shop is open and pay for rental gear, and no rushing to return the equipment to avoid extra fees. Owning does entail some responsibility, though. You need to maintain your own gear. That means rinsing, drying, and seeing that it is serviced on a regular basis. These costs need to be considered as well unless you service your own, which some divers do. Owning your own equipment may be right for you. On the other hand, it could be that renting is the best option. Having never rented, I am somewhat biased towards owning gear. I therefore asked a friend to explain her reasons for not owning all her own gear. Here is her response to the question:

My original decision was to own all the personal gear, including exposure protection, and to rent all of the equipment (BC, regulator, console) when diving. I have tended to be a once-yearly vacation diver with just a rare local dive for refresher purposes, and it didn't make sense to me to invest in equipment that would sit around taking up space most of the time, but which would still have maintenance requirements. After I got a few dives under my belt, I decided I wanted to start using a computer and immediately bought one; I didn't want to have to learn a new computer every time I went diving, so renting one didn't look tempting. Having lived with my original decisions now for nearly a decade, I can say they have worked out very well for me and I wouldn't change a thing.

Buying the personal gear has been a very good investment. I like having reliable fit every time I put on my mask, and in my case, it's a must because of prescription lenses. Having my own booties and fins means I never have to worry about chafing or poor fit, so I'm happy that I have those. Knowing my computer is a safety essential for me, so I'd never rent one unless I had no choice. I find having my own pieces of these particular bits of gear to be worth the trouble of carrying them when I travel. They weigh something, to be sure, and the fins dictate the dimensions of the luggage I must use, but the trade-off is worthwhile for me.

Because I require a lot of exposure protection, my exposure suit (7mm) is a real pain for travel. It's heavy, takes up a lot of room in the luggage, and can be difficult to get dried out in time for getting stuffed into the luggage for the trip home. However, taking my own is the only way I can guarantee a good fit, and frankly, the rental suits I've seen often look kind of gross.

I have never regretted renting BCs and regulators/consoles at my destination. The rentals have always been in really nice shape (with one exception which looked sad but was functional and safe) and have worked properly. I don't have to make room for them in luggage, carry their weight, worry about getting them dried out for the trip home, clean them when I get home, or spend time or money on maintenance. Because I rent, I seem to always have pretty up-to-date gear. In all these years, my rental charges would probably equal the cost of a BC that would have been recommended at the beginning. By now, I'd have broken even financially or might even be ahead, but would have a ten-year-old BC instead of the fairly new ones I use each time.

More local diving options have recently become available to me, so when I had a chance at a nicely priced, used BC, I jumped on it. I paid less for it than two rentals, so even if I never use it again, I'm already ahead. I could take this BC on

151

trips and would enjoy having a familiar BC with me, but I probably won't. Taking it would still require a lot of extra effort on my part, plus the BC would be exposed to seawater, which would involve a LOT of post-trip maintenance. I'd rather just enjoy my trip without worrying about equipment, and walk away with only my personal gear to clean up at home. Same with a regulator; I'd rather leave the maintenance and storage to someone else.

Here, you have a compelling argument for only owning the basic personal gear that is well thought out and makes a great deal of sense. There are some for whom renting gear is a genuinely better option, especially when a detailed cost/benefit analysis has been considered. In the end, it all comes down to what is best for you and your diving style. It also helps if your wallet is happy with the decision you make when you go to the dive shop.

Notes

Chapter Thirteen
Why Dive Locally?

As one who began his dive career in a lake with poor visibility on its *good* days, I am now going to delve into an area that is getting less and less attention from the dive industry. While many of us end up doing checkout dives in a lake or quarry, the new diver is often bombarded with images of oceans and warm water as the norm for diving. There are enough books, articles, and websites dealing with the ocean and its many wonders. I'm going to try to reveal the wonder and attraction of our other bodies of water, those that tend to be freshwater, inland, and much closer to many of our homes.

Some consider local diving as little more than a last resort, assuming that all they can look forward to is low visibility, cold water, few fish, and barren landscapes. Many divers, however, actually appreciate local diving as their preference for experiencing the underwater world. Local diving can offer sights that those who only do warm-water resort dives will never see. Saltwater is quite harsh on most materials, while freshwater is much more forgiving. As a result, shipwrecks last much longer in freshwater than they do in saltwater and other manmade structures do, as well. Bridges and even buildings can be found in some freshwater lakes created by flooding as a result of dams. There are underwater forests containing trees with branches, with fish instead of leaves among those branches. In addition to the sights, there are the very real advantages of not having salt infiltrate every nook and cranny of the dive gear and the diver!

I am a huge supporter of local diving and what it does for divers and dive shops. Local divers enjoy a number of benefits that are obvious and a few that are not. The most obvious benefit is the cost of travel to the site. Airfares can add up quickly, and as of this writing we also need to deal with the intrusiveness of full body scans and "enhanced pat-downs" bordering on sexual assault by low paid, poorly trained, and sometimes insensitive Transportation Security Administration (TSA) agents. Local diving allows us to avoid all of this. For a few dollars in fuel, a little time in the car, and no scrutiny other than that of your dive buddies, you're diving! Local diving can be as simple as deciding to dive, calling a buddy or even a group of divers, and getting the gear together. You then plan the dive or dives, do them, and either go home for a relaxing evening or get together with your buddies for some good times afterwards. No airports, no hotel reservations, and no huge logistical challenges. In addition, access to sites is often as simple as driving up to the shore and setting up gear. There is no need to load and unload a boat, or to wait for other divers to start the dive planning process. Some inland dive sites have facilities for changing, taking a shower, using the restroom, and even getting air fills. A number of privately owned quarries are set up as dive sites; they do charge admission, but it is still nowhere near the cost of a boat ride in a tropical location. The money they collect is used to maintain the facility and add attractions both above and below the water to make the whole SCUBA diving experience as pleasant as possible.

Dive Site Amenities and Attractions

These attractions include sunken boats, buses, trucks, airplanes and helicopters. Large iron or concrete pipes are often put in place to create swim-throughs or overhead environments for advanced and technical training. Many facilities install platforms for use in training. Even though divers should not be kneeling on these, the platforms are helpful as the bottoms of these quarries are often quite silty. Performing drills over a silty bottom, especially with newer divers, can have adverse effects on visibility; performing those same drills over a wooden or metal platform greatly reduces this problem. Placing these platforms takes time, money, and the efforts of divers who often volunteer to assist in their construction. They do this to practice skills, provide themselves with places to train, and to give other divers a place to use. Some facilities install whimsical features like underwater cemeteries that they "decorate" for Halloween, or they will have Santa and his reindeer for the viewing pleasure of those who love cold-water diving. Some allow divers to bring their own objects to place on the bottom, for numerous reasons. More than a few of these sites have memorial plaques for friends who have passed, who loved the sport. Everything described in this paragraph gets done by those who love diving and wish to see it grow and continue. Divers tend to be very unselfish and caring people.

Many local dive sites have personnel on hand to assist with emergencies. In addition, inland freshwater sites are usually no more than minutes away from actual emergency response units with ambulances, helicopters, and hospital facilities. The ocean, while beautiful, often requires longer response times due to the sheer distances involved. In dive emergencies, time is critical for successful outcomes. The local dive site, with or without its own facilities, can be a literal life saver in that we have faster access to care.

Along with underwater attractions, air fills, showers, and quick access to care, many inland dive sites also offer camping facilities and/or on-site concession stands for food and drink. While these stands will never be confused with five-star restaurants, the food they have is generally good, hot, and filling, which are the three most important things this diver looks for. Those that have camping facilities may also include cabins. They're not the Ritz, but they're still better than a tent, back seat of a car, or bed of a pickup truck. Finally, for those who want to stay overnight in somewhat cushier accommodations, many inland sites have agreements with local hotels to provide rooms at reduced rates for divers. These hotels realize the value of catering to divers. Many of us are non-smokers, tend to be more respectful of others' property, have little need for fancy amenities, and have a little money to spend. All of these are excellent guest characteristics that are well-appreciated by anyone in the hospitality business. If you belong to AAA, their discount sometimes beats the rates local quarries have negotiated with neighboring hotels. It always pays to investigate these deals.

Local Diving is Family-Friendly

Another consideration involves those of us who have non-diving spouses or families; inland sites often offer attractions for them as well. Many have constructed beaches, play areas for children, waterslides, and other recreational opportunities such as kayaking and tubing. I know of one site that even has a climbing wall
for guests to use. Operators of these sites recognize the importance of family support when it comes to SCUBA diving. The diver who is always leaving the spouse and kids at home soon finds out that diving is not as enjoyable nor as tolerated when loved ones can't be involved.

Diving can be a fantastic family activity even if the whole family does not dive; the important thing is to get the family involved in some way. Local diving is an economical way to do this, and older kids make great gear Sherpas, carrying tanks, weights, assisting with BC straps, etc. It gets them involved and perhaps even interested in diving for themselves. The parent who gets their kids involved in a positive experience like SCUBA diving is not only getting them interested in a good, wholesome activity, but is also reinforcing family bonds. I recently taught an entire family to dive. To see the interaction and closeness they shared when they were training and to now see them capably planning and doing actual dives together is one of the most gratifying experiences for me as an instructor. Local diving also allows the family to take a mini-vacation, if you will, and not have to rush for airports, rearrange schedules, or lose time from school studies. In the long days of late summer and early fall, the kids can get out of school, get with their parents, and in as little as an hour, be at a local site for a couple dives and perhaps a picnic supper. Not many have the opportunity to share that kind of enjoyable, unique experience together, with all of the distractions families have today. Underwater, as a family in the world of solitude and neutral buoyancy they create, they can connect with each other and also detach from the pressures of school, work, and the world in general. Learning about the underwater environment and themselves, together with the closeness diving brings, they strengthen family bonds and discover how much they can rely on each other.

Local Diving Builds Your Skills

For the diver as an individual, the educational benefits of diving locally cannot be underestimated. It is in our local lakes and quarries that skills are honed and polished. I am of the opinion that every dive is a skills dive; each time I go underwater, I decide on a skill for practice. Even if it's only for ten minutes during a one hour dive, I will work on buoyancy, trim, propulsion, or some other aspect of my diving. The good diver is always looking to improve skills, safety, and enjoyment. When you decide that you need to get just a bit better in one area or another, you take more responsibility for yourself and ultimately for the people you will dive with. The local dive site is the place where you can do this. You call a buddy and ask them to come with you for a dive to work on skills. You have no planes to catch, no TSA groping, no reservations to make, and no big schedule changes to make. You just go and dive. When you do this, you have total control over time, depth, and course. It affords you the opportunity to keep skills sharp and up-to-date for that next big trip. We often go on trips to exotic places and see divers who, frankly, are pretty frightening in their lack of skills and knowledge. We often find out that they only dive on vacation, would never get in their local watering hole, and often do not have their own equipment. They have not even done a refresher since the last dive a year or more ago. Yet here they are, seemingly oblivious to the concerns and dangers inherent in diving. What is worse is *we may be asked to buddy up with these people and possibly rely on them in an emergency*. If you are asked to do this, you are well within your rights to say, "No, thank you." You are never obligated to dive with anyone whose skills or practices make you uncomfortable.

The educational portion of local diving begins in the classroom and pool. If a student will be doing checkout dives in a local quarry or lake, they should be learning the benefits of doing so from the very beginning. The instructor should be priming the student to think about all the great things to be seen and done at local dive sites, with focus on what a good opportunity it is for working on buoyancy, trim, propulsion, and basic skills. It should be pointed out that one can do all these things and not have to worry about strong currents, waves, or dangerous marine life. By the time my students get to their OW checkout dives, they are truly excited about seeing a bluegill or catfish, and the idea of just being underwater outside of a swimming pool. If your instructor does not have you feeling the same way, I can only say I feel sorry for you and your instructor. There is that much to be excited about. Divers who feel that excitement are the divers who will practice regularly, becoming both safer and safer to be with. They are also the divers who will get the most enjoyment from diving, wherever they go.

You don't always need to be under the direction of an instructor to improve your skills. One of the most valuable things you can do is find a mentor. A mentor will be the experienced diver (or divers) often found at local sites, dive clubs or even at local dive shops. They are the ones who will take you under their wing (or fin) and show you the fine points of the basics you have just been taught. There is a finite amount of time that an instructor can spend with a student and a limited amount of time in most classes to practice skills. This is where actually getting out and diving completes the training cycle. You could continue to take course after course and get extra time with a professional but the truth is that this is not necessary. It can also get quite expensive. Partnering with a mentor usually will cost no more than it takes to just go dive. Although, if a diver is spending time working on your skills with you, showing you the area, and helping to increase your enjoyment and safety, the least you can do is buy him or her lunch! My own mentor was not a professional and did not have thousands of dives. What he did have was a deep love for diving and the importance of skills. His navigational skills were uncanny and to this day I still strive to emulate them. This is perhaps the greatest benefit of mentors: They encourage and help us to develop our own abilities, while inspiring us to do better, appreciate the sport, and in many cases put in us that spark to help others as we ourselves have been helped. This is hard to find on a dive boat with strangers you will most likely never see again. At the local dive site, however, there are those who will not only

159

become mentors who you will see on a regular basis, they will also become friends who may last a lifetime

If you enjoy photography, there should be a great deal of practice in holding trim and buoyancy while stationary, along with using back kicks and precise turns to track your subject. With digital underwater cameras, you can practice as much as you like and take as many shots as you wish. In photography competitions, local freshwater photos are often a category that gets less interest than others, so the chance to win is greater. If reef ecology is your thing, taking time to study and document the local fish population can be good practice. Combine this with a call to your local or state Conservation or Fish and Game agency to see if they would be interested in your observations, or to provide some information about local species. The skills necessary for this include navigating to a site, holding position in the water column, and documenting a sighting on a slate or in wetnotes. With a bit of imagination and commitment on your part, the opportunities to improve your knowledge and skills are almost limitless. Imagine the school bus is a shipwreck and it becomes one. See the manmade swim-through as a real one in a coral reef and you will work on not touching the sides. Take the time to learn the little nuances and quirks of your local sites. You may begin to love the idea of local diving as much as I do.

Local Diving has Fewer Risks

Another advantage of the local dive site is that there are very few things that can hurt us there -- no great whites, stinging jellyfish, venomous fish, or giant squid. Catfish generally stay away, so other than the occasional aggressive, four-inch bluegill protecting its eggs, there is very little to be concerned with as far as hazardous marine life. Unlike the ocean, many local quarries used for diver training do not allow fishing, so there is no entanglement concern with monofilament line. Most freshwater lakes do allow fishing, but it is often in an area that divers do not frequent. No fishing also means no boats or irresponsible boat operators to worry about -- another plus to diving locally. Where divers and boats do mix, there are numerous incidents and close calls, often involving alcohol. It is an unfortunate fact that in these events, the diver is at a distinct disadvantage; anything that reduces or eliminates this risk is a very good thing. In short, the biggest danger of most local dive sites is often the drive to the site; the prepared, skilled, and knowledgeable diver has little to fear. This is not to say we should lose respect for what we are doing and the environment we are going to be in. Local diving is still diving, with all the physiological risks inherent to the sport, but it allows for the reduction of certain external risks and provides a more controlled environment than is possible in ocean diving.

The Big-Picture Economic Benefits of Local Diving

Now, let's look at the benefits of local diving for the local dive shop, the local economy, and the dive industry as a whole. As has been stated previously, the dive shop is often the first point of contact for the new diver. It is where most divers get their first concrete impressions about SCUBA diving and is often the deciding factor in whether they continue to dive after their initial certification. Many shops would not even exist but for the presence of local dive opportunities. The dive shop is a business that needs to make money to survive; they do this primarily by providing training and selling equipment. Most shop owners will admit that training is not their primary source of revenue. Some shops manage to turn out large numbers of divers or charge more for the courses they offer, but even then, a great deal of expense is involved with training divers. Pool time, equipment and compressor maintenance, insurance, staff pay, etc. are all costs borne by the shop. The price of the OW class today in many areas is not what it should be but it is what the public, for now, will bear. Broken down to an hourly rate, the OW class should be much more expensive than it is, given what it does. Teaching people to survive, play, and have fun safely in an environment that is hostile to human life is a serious undertaking, involving a great deal of time and commitment on the part of the instructor. Rarely are instructors paid what they are truly worth.

So where *does* the shop look to for revenue? From sales of equipment -- that is where the money comes in, and local divers spend a lot of money on gear. Vacation divers may buy a BC or regulator, and perhaps an exposure suit. Often they do not, as it is easier to rent everything when they get to their destination. While vacation divers do or should own their personal gear (mask, snorkel, fins, boots), shops cannot survive on this and neither can the industry as a whole. Local divers buy BCs, regulators, suits, tanks, weights, numerous accessories, and pay for air fills – this is what keeps the shop in business. The smart dive shop will put a great deal of focus on serving and meeting the needs of its local divers. They will keep prices fair and competitive. They will have hours convenient for the local diving population. They will stock what local divers need and want in the way of products and brands; most of all, they will provide good service for those items. If they do this, the divers will come and more importantly, they will come back again and again. The smart dive shop realizes that they're unlikely to see much of their students after certification unless they help those students to appreciate the benefits of diving locally. Getting divers interested in local sites ensures that they will at some point wish to own their own equipment, as rental costs begin to add up. Divers may also soon see the benefits of using gear they know, which is always available, and is serviced as they know it should be. To ignore the local diver is one very good way of committing business suicide. No one wants to see any business fail, but to see it fail because it ignored the best source of its support is even more tragic. When any local dive shop fails, the whole industry suffers.

The dive industry, specifically the manufacturers, is dependent on the survival of local dive shops and sales of equipment through them. When a shop fails, that is less revenue for the supplier. Simple economics tells us that if suppliers lose a resource to market their goods, they have less opportunity to sell those goods. Fewer sales mean less money for research and development of new products. This results in even fewer sales because no one wants to replace what they already have if it works well. New features and designs attract buyers. For example, your car runs well and gets you where you are going. So why do you want a new one? Well, the new one has the Super XT package and it's better. Why? Not sure, but it looks better, so it must be. SCUBA gear and gear purchasers are no different. Yes, there are some features that are very nice to have and do enhance the experience, but gear is all basically the same. If there was no money for R&D and the manufacturers only had a few outlets for their products, we would surely not have the variety of choices we do today. So, a healthy dive shop that has local divers supporting it has a direct effect on the health of the equipment manufacturers.

Local diving is the basis for the health of the entire industry. It all begins with the diver who gets certified, buys his or her own equipment, and jumps into the local watering hole. The resorts

163

are even dependent, in a roundabout way, on local divers who never show up on their doorstep. The local diver helps keep the doors of the local dive shop open; that dive shop is therefore available to offer the vacation diver the chance to get certified. This allows the newly minted vacation diver to be able to book a trip to the resort and provide income for the resort. The local dive shop that entices students only with visions of exotic, warm-water locations shows an example of the backwards thinking that is common in dive training today. When divers are trained with the expectation that they will always be going *away* to dive, the local dive shop loses a great opportunity, perhaps several. They cannot or will not see that the vacation diver is often a one-shot deal. Many are not, but enough are that if they were persuaded into trying local diving, the local dive shop could reap substantial benefits and revenue. The focus on travel and exotic destinations which is practiced by many in the industry is, in my opinion, very shortsighted and self-defeating. There is a movement to change this and I fully support it.

The final benefit of local diving is to the local economy as whole. When local divers buy gasoline, a sandwich or a soda at the gas station, or stop for lunch at a local restaurant, they are supporting the people who live and work nearby. They provide the opportunity for their neighbors to be employed. The sales tax they pay on the gear at the local dive shop supports their local community and helps maintain the infrastructure of that area. Local divers who are active are often seen as being more responsible people; those who foster and nurture that image may make it easier to get access for others divers to more sites. Local divers organize and participate in volunteer efforts to clean and maintain waterways; there are various clean-up projects available for those who wish to help. In addition, that kind of volunteering is another opportunity to get in the water and improve the image of diving. The media often focus on negative events connected to diving: drownings, shark attacks, missing divers, and the like. It is not often that other stories get told. If local diving starts to get the attention from the industry that it deserves, it may start to get positive media attention as well. That would be a very good thing for the local dive shop, the manufacturers, and especially those of us who truly love the challenges and wonders of the local environment.

In conclusion, I would like to give to you who have purchased and read this work, my deepest and heartfelt thanks. I hope you have found it informative, thought-provoking, and useful. It is and has been my sole intention since becoming a dive professional, to see that the person who undertakes this sport does so in a skilled, informed, and most of all, safe manner. Up until now, the only way I could do this was in my own classes, in conversation with other divers, and through various message boards. These have brought me great personal satisfaction, new friends, and some praise from what I consider to be great people in the diving community. But it was still lacking in that I could not seem to address all of the issues I wanted to, and say everything I wanted to say. I'm sure that as soon as this book is out and in distribution, I will run into situations where I need to say more. Maybe that will be the next book. Until then, I hope that you take the information here and use it to increase your enjoyment of, knowledge of, and most of all, safe pursuit of exploration of the underwater universe on SCUBA.

©2010 James A Lapenta -Coral formations, Puerto Rico

Chapter Fourteen
Basic Gear Maintenance
2nd Edition Bonus Chapter

Everyone has their own comfort level when it comes to how far they want to go in taking care of their dive gear. That said, the more basic maintenance you are able to perform, the less likely it is that a small problem will ruin your dive day. That is what this section is about – basic maintenance. I am not going to tell you how to tear down and service your own regulator or even the power inflator on your BC. Those are jobs for trained technicians, though you will hear of some divers who do these tasks themselves.

Please note that as an Equipment Technician and Technician Instructor, I do not encourage you to do advanced work on your gear. Should you choose to do so, be advised that you will likely void any warranty or free parts program that may be in place for your equipment, and that you do so entirely at your own risk of serious injury or even death.

What I *will* talk about are those steps that you can take to extend the life of your gear. Some of this you will have been taught in your initial training, while some is likely new to you. In today's model of short classes and reduced face time with an instructor, this kind of information is sometimes being left out. It seems as if it's just, "Rinse it, dry it, and don't leave it in the sun," and other very general information that is casually passed on. As a technician, I see the effects of this on a regular basis, often resulting in the need for remedies that are costly in both parts and labor. For the diver on a budget, that is never a good thing. So let's take a look at what you can do to save money, extend the life of your gear, ensure you do not miss dives, and most of all decrease your risk of an equipment issue that could jeopardize your safety.

We'll start with your regulator. In general your regulator is a robust, well-engineered, and time tested device that allows you to breathe underwater. I am not going get deeply into regulator theory here as there are already numerous references available that do a fine job of it. The short version though is that the modern SCUBA regulator is used to reduce high pressure air at the first stage to what is known as an intermediate pressure, which is delivered to the second stages. The second stages then allow divers to breathe air at the ambient pressure of their current depth. That's it in a nutshell. To do that, a combination of springs, diaphragms, seats, adjusting screws, orifices, and some internal design are brought into play. Our focus is on what you can do to make sure this keeps happening reliably.

The first is inspecting your gear before each dive and looking at a few basic items. *This applies to gear you may rent as well. Do not put all your faith in the provider of that equipment telling you that everything is fine! As a certified diver you are responsible to make sure that your gear is working and safe to dive.* The first item you want to look at is the overall condition of the regulator. Does it appear to be clean and free of corrosion? There should not be anything green and fuzzy growing on it. Do the hoses appear new and supple with no cracks or dry rot in evidence? Pull back the hose protectors and make sure the fittings are not corroded. Many experienced divers don't use hose protectors because they hide problems and can also trap dirt, sand, and salt. Make sure there are no unusual bulges, and in the case of braided type hoses, no fraying of the outer case.

Push the purge buttons on the second stages. Are they smooth and free of sticking? Is there any sign of excess wear or cracking of the cover? If so, bring it to the attention of the shop and ask for a new setup. If it's your own gear then have it looked at and any worn items replaced. Now take the dust cap off of the first stage and inspect the filter in the inlet that connects to the tank. Unless the regulator has an auto-closing device that supposedly keeps water from accidentally intruding into the first stage, you should be able to see the filter. It will be silver or gold in color. It should never be green or black, or show signs of corrosion. If it does, that indicates a problem in the maintenance of the regulator or the air supply that it has been hooked up to at some point. Such a unit should not be used until it has been properly serviced to resolve the problem.

Now, put the regulator on a tank, purge the second stages, then exhale sharply though each of them to check that the exhaust diaphragms are not sticking. This also helps to ensure you do not swallow anything that may have crawled into the regulator while it was not being used! Next, just breathe it and watch the pressure gauge to make sure the gauge is working.

Ensure that the connection on the LP inflator hose works freely when you pull it back and release it. Finally, check that the submersible pressure gauge swivels freely. After the dive is where you make all the difference in how the regulator behaves the next time. Proper rinsing is your responsibility!

Proper rinsing procedures start out the same whether you've used the regulator in saltwater or fresh, but there are some additional concerns with saltwater units that we'll get to in a minute. All regulators should be thoroughly rinsed with running water. It is common practice for divers to swish their gear in a dunk tank, take it all out and then leave it hanging to dry. The problem with this is that after one diver rinses gear in it, the water in the dunk tank is no longer clean. It's water now holding in suspension the salt, debris, and dirt from the gear of every diver who got there before you. A dunk tank is okay to loosen things up but it is not a substitute for properly rinsing your gear. Proper rinsing involves taking the regulator while still hooked up to an air supply, running fresh water over the first stage, and then rinsing the second stages with that same running water. Press the purge buttons while doing this. Make sure that the exhaust diaphragms are free of debris and sediment. Just put a thumb over the mouthpiece as you purge and direct the air out through the exhaust. Then you can turn the air supply off, depressurize the regulator, and remove it from the air supply. Now it is ready to be hung to dry.

For regulators used in saltwater, I recommend a few extra steps, especially if a regulator is used on a trip and then brought home. This is where, as a technician, I most often run into extra work. The dunk tanks at nearly every operation I have been to are nothing more than miniature oceans. The water in them might get changed twice a day, if at all. As such, they don't get gear clean. They do, however, introduce even finer versions of salt, sand, silt, etc. to the regulator and other gear. What I advise divers to do if the tanks are not constantly refilled with fresh water is to take the regulator off of the tank, dry the dust cap, and then take it to your room. Once back at the room make sure the dust cap is in place, drape it around your neck, and take it into the shower with you. Rinse the first stage, then the second stages while depressing the purges a few times, and exhale through them. This allows warm running water to dissolve and rinse away the salt and other crud. Then hang the regulator on the towel bar and finish your shower. If there are hose protectors, pull them back and allow the regulator to dry before putting them back in place. When you get home from the trip, if the regulator will not be used again soon, repeat the shower steps or fill the kitchen sink with warm water, and soak the second stages. Do not press the purges unless you have a tank to hook the regulator up to. Rinse the first stage with the dust cap in place under the tap, then change the water and repeat. Allow the regulator to dry thoroughly and then store out of direct sunlight.

I have a pet peeve about how drying the dust cap is taught to many new divers. I was taught to dry the dust cap by cracking open the tank valve and using the tank air to dry the cap. In my opinion, this is the worst way to do it, because you risk directing water from the dust cap directly into the first stage at very high pressure. If the dust cap is not fastened to the first stage you risk blowing it away and into the dirt, or overboard if on a boat. The other problem this presents is, just how far do you open the valve? For some, it's just the tiniest crack that does the job and is fairly unobtrusive. Others seem to feel that they must open the valve all the way, which is how you risk the water intrusion and loss of the cap. Not to mention that it is very unnerving to be next to someone who suddenly does this and scares the pants off of you! Finally, the noise from this is actually painful for some people. Please do yourself and other divers a big favor – use a towel, corner of your shirt, or some other clean cloth to dry the dust cap, not the air from the tank.

Now we'll look at your buoyancy compensator (BC). There are some important items to consider. First, do the inflator buttons work smoothly? Are they overly stiff or so easy that they feel sloppy? Either can be a problem underwater. Too stiff and they may cause inflation or deflation issues. Too loose and they may leak; it could mean an O-ring is compromised depending on the style of inflator. Check the corrugated hose and the LP hose connection on the inflator unit. The LP connection is something that can loosen and may need tightening. A small crescent wrench is usually sufficient to remedy this and there are also inexpensive, specialized tools available for taking care of many inflator issues. If the BC is equipped with a pull dump on the inflator hose, check its operation. This can be done by orally inflating the BC and tugging on the hose; it should not take great effort to do this. The operation should be smooth and immediate. If it isn't, get it checked. Next, check any additional dump valves on the unit and ensure that they work as intended. These are also over-pressure relief valves and by hooking the BC up to a tank, you can inflate the BC until the valves activate. If they don't, do not dive the unit until you've had the valves checked. Make sure the BC holds air and listen for leaks. Check all the straps, assuring that none are frayed or cut, and that they adjust as they should. Check all the releases and buckles, and inspect them for cracks or missing parts.

If you have a weight-integrated BC, carefully inspect the pockets for bad Velcro, loose fasteners, cracked plastic, and

170

rips or tears. If you find any, don't trust the pockets with your weights -- replace them. I do not recommend repair of weight pockets unless done by the factory. Next, take a look at the tank cam straps. There should be no fraying and the buckles should show no cracks or other structural issues. The overall appearance of the BC is somewhat open to personal preference. Some divers like their gear to look as if it just came out of the showroom, while others feel some fading and staining give it character. In either case there should be no tears, rips, loose piping or trim. Any irregularity or defect that could compromise the integrity of the unit should be dealt with before using it.

Caring for your BC is not difficult and involves little more than careful rinsing and drying. Again, you want to avoid communal dunk tanks! Rinse it with a hose or, if on a trip, in the shower with you. A hose is better as it allows you to rinse the inflator while working the buttons. Try to get some fresh water into the bladder and once you do, orally inflate the BC. Turn it upside down, shake it to rinse the inner walls of the bladder, then drain the unit via the inflator and dump valves. Do this a few times and then partially inflate the BC for storage. This works for wings as well if you happen to dive a back plate and wing. If the BC has pockets, open them and rinse them out. Rinse the weight pockets as well and allow them to dry before reinstalling them in the BC. Rinse the additional dump valves with running water while operating them. If the BC has been used in a pool, rinse the entire rig thoroughly; chlorine can cause premature fading of the material. Whether to store the BC hanging or lying flat is one of those things where opinions differ. If the unit is thoroughly dry and not going into long term storage, being flat is not that big a deal. BCs are tough. Personally I feel that hanging it up, partially inflated and in a cool dry environment out of direct sun, is the best way to store a BC. It ensures that no mold or mildew is going to form from moisture that may have gotten trapped somewhere in it. It also ensures that no unusual folds or creases affect the bladder. This is my own preference and I have found it the best way for my gear.

Some other common items I get asked about caring for are lights, reels, spools, surface marker buoys (SMBs), slates and other small accessories. For the most part, all that is required is careful rinsing and drying, but I feel a few items should be addressed here based on personal experience. The first is lights.

Photo by James Lapenta © 2013

I have a number of lights, from small backups costing less than $30 to canister lights used for technical dives that retail for over $1000. One thing that they all have in common are those little pieces of rubber or silicone known as O-rings; bad O-rings result in flooding of the light. They get nicked, cut, dried out, or in some cases, left on the bench or counter at home. Any of these scenarios can pretty much guarantee you'll be buying a new light after it floods, but they can be prevented quite easily. It is simply a matter of taking a few minutes after each dive day, rinsing and drying the light, and then taking it apart, inspecting it, and lubricating the O-rings with the proper silicone grease as recommended by the manufacturer. That's it. Inspecting involves drying them with a lint free cloth and checking the entire ring. If it's nicked or cut, replace it. While you have the light apart, clean and inspect the threads on the cap and light body. The lint free cloth should be used here as well. A thin film of lube on the threads is a good idea, *but be careful as the threads are often precision made and sharp enough to cut a finger!* For lubricating the threads, an old toothbrush reserved for the job works well. When lubricating O-rings, be very careful not to overdo it; too much will trap dirt and sand. All you need is a thin sheen of lube. What I do is dip my index finger in the lube, rub that with my thumb a couple of times, then roll the O-ring between my thumb and index finger. That is all that's required. If your light has mechanical switches, inspect them and if they have a screw holding the switch on, check it. Personal experience with this is why I no longer use lights that have a screw holding the switch on.

Photos Courtesy of Edge Gear

Reels and spools range from finger spools that can be had for under $20, to expedition-grade reels costing a few hundred. One thing they all have in common is the line they hold. Over time with repeated use, line gets frayed, twisted, knotted and can be compromised with foreign objects. This can be inconvenient for the recreational diver, but for the technical diver it can literally be a death sentence. Based on your own usage, a schedule should be set up to inspect the line for frays, cuts, knots, or foreign objects that may be trapped in it. If you find any issues at all, I recommend only one thing -- replace the line, in its entirety. DO NOT splice new line onto the reel or spool. Line is inexpensive and splicing just introduces another defect. There are various ways to inspect your line. Coiling it into a bucket works well. What I sometimes do if the weather permits is tie off my spools and reels outside and run them all the way out in my yard. I will even set up stakes and practice tie offs while doing this to keep it off the ground. It's also fun to see the reactions of the neighbors!

In the case of reels you should inspect the handle, winding crank, set screw, and the spool itself. Any observed defects should be addressed and taken care of before using it again. With reels there is another item to consider and that is the quality of the reel itself. Personal experience has taught me that going cheap is very expensive. Reels with gimmicks such as ratchets also tend to add to maintenance issues and problems with usage. My experience is that when I made the mistake of choosing between a $100 reel and a similar one costing half as much, I bought the cheaper one but ended up paying for both. I had to buy the $100 reel anyway after the cheaper one fell apart the fourth time I had it in the water. There are some items you can get away with going for a "bargain," so to speak. Reels, in my opinion, are not one of those. Spend the extra money to reduce long term costs on a good reel. There are many of them out there in the $75-$100 price range which will serve the recreational diver well.

Photo by James A Lapenta © 2013

A surface marker buoy (SMB) is a valuable safety item and, when coupled with a reel or spool, provides the diver with a visual and tactile reference underwater. This is especially important in cases where a team of divers misses the mooring or anchor line at the end of the dive and needs to make a free or "blue water" ascent. The SMB is nothing more than an inflatable fabric tube, differing from a safety sausage in that it has an overpressure relief valve to allow it to be inflated and deployed from depth without rupturing.

Caring for the SMB is similar to the BC. Rinsing, inflating, and checking the dump or overpressure valve (OPV) is the same. You must assure that the OPV operates perfectly, because a stuck OPV can cause the tube to rupture or be impossible to inflate as it continually dumps air put into it. A faulty inflator on a closed-bottomed SMB can make it impossible to inflate the tube. Always carefully rinse both the OPV and the inflator with running water and operate them as you do so. Once you have done this, hang the SMB and partially inflate it. Allow it to dry thoroughly and then store it as recommended.

Slates are another item I get asked about. What's the best way to clean them? Spending a little extra money on a good hard slate makes cleaning easier. A standard gum rubber eraser from any office supply store will do the job. Cheaper slates made of softer plastic end up getting scratched up, scored, and become a nightmare to clean. With these, the best thing I have found is the rubber eraser coupled with a mild abrasive cleaner like Soft

Scrub or the cheap toothpaste you find at dollar stores. At some point, though, you will end up replacing the slate as it just gets too bad and can't be gotten clean. This is when I usually advise divers to replace the slate with an underwater note book. These allow for recording more detailed information and are refillable with waterproof paper.

I hope that this short section on maintaining your equipment is useful to you and answers questions you may have had. Please feel free to contact me for more detailed or item-specific suggestions and advice.

Appendix A:
SCUBA Terms

Every sport involves terminology and some slang that is
particular to that sport. In the case of SCUBA diving, some
terms may vary by region, agency, and even instructor. While
it's not possible to cover all SCUBA terms here, the following
list covers the most common, including short, additional
descriptions where necessary.

AAUS -- American Academy of Underwater Sciences.
Establishes guidelines and standards for a number of
scientific diving programs which are used at universities,
research programs, and some public aquariums.

ACUC -- American Canadian Underwater Certification.
A training agency.

Advanced Dive – A dive beyond the recommended limits
for an OW diver, or one that requires more than basic skills.
Deep dives, night dives, navigation, search and recovery,
and drift dives are commonly called Advanced Dives.

Agency – Instructors are certified to teach through an
agency when they agree to abide by and are trained to the
standards of that agency. Once the diver has met those
requirements, the agency issues the certification.

AOW – Advanced Open Water. The AOW course takes
many forms depending on the instructor, and agency
standards. It implies that divers have been given training
beyond the basic OW course and are therefore qualified to
do more advanced dives. Many dive operators will require
an AOW card for certain dives to reduce their risk of
liability.

Archimedes' Principle – Describes buoyancy as the
amount of buoyant (upward) force on an object in a liquid,
as determined by the amount of liquid displaced by the
object.

Artificial Reef – Any object or objects that have been placed by man to add to the natural environment as a habitat for marine life. These often result in new locations for divers and fishermen as well. The most well-known artificial reefs are decommissioned military ships intentionally sunk for this purpose (after thorough cleaning).

Ascent – The process of going up in the water column.

ATA – Acronym for Atmosphere Absolute. It is the depth plus the pressure of the air on the surface.

Atmosphere – A unit used to describe the amount of pressure per square inch exerted on an object. The surface (14.7 psi) is one atmosphere or **ATA**. Each 33 feet of seawater (FSW) or 34 feet of freshwater (FFW) adds an additional **ATA** of pressure. For example, the pressure at 33 FSW equals two atmospheres or 2 **ATA**.

Back Inflate BC – A **BC** with the air bladder mounted on the rear of the unit.

Backplate and Wing – Also known as a BPW, a modular type of **BC** that is made up of a stainless steel, aluminum, or kydex plate with a harness, and a detachable **bladder (wing)** that is favored by technical divers and recreational divers who prefer a simplistic type of buoyancy control.

Backward Roll – A type of entry where the diver simply rolls backwards off of a boat or dock.

Balanced Regulator – A regulator first stage designed to deliver a constant flow of air at any depth regardless of tank pressure.

Balanced Rig – A balanced rig is used to describe a diver's SCUBA setup when proper weighting has been established. The diver should be weighted so that if the **BC** fails, it is still possible to swim the unit to the surface.

BAR – A metric measure of pressure, used instead of psi.

Barotrauma – Term used to describe injury caused by pressure changes.

BC or BCD – Acronym for Buoyancy Compensator or Buoyancy Compensation Device.

Bioprene – A slang term used to describe the diver's own body fat.

Bladder – The part of the **BC** that actually holds the air or other breathing gas.

Bottom Time – Most often defined as beginning when the diver leaves the surface, and ending when they begin their ascent or reach their safety stop.

Bottom Timer – A digital or analog device that keeps track of a diver's time underwater. Digital timers may also have features such as depth, an ascent rate indicator, and the ability to keep track of the dive, but do not track nitrogen loading (for that, you need a **computer**).

Boyle's Law – A law describing the relationship between pressure and volume. As pressure increases, volume decreases.

BSAC – British Sub Aqua Club. A club-based certification agency, primarily in the United Kingdom.

Buddy – A dive partner.

Buddy Breathing – A valuable skill that is no longer taught by many agencies at the Open Water level. It involves divers sharing one second stage, alternately taking two breaths each while swimming or ascending. Used when one diver has run out of air or suffered a loss of air supply.

Buddy Skills – The ability of divers to maintain contact, communicate, and assist each other on a dive.

Buddy System - First used by the **YMCA** swim program in the USA, it was later adapted and carried over when the **YMCA** became the first national **SCUBA** training program. Based on the idea that divers should never dive alone, it is a key component of any dive and dive planning.

Buoyancy Compensator – A device that allows a diver to control his or her place in the water column by adding and subtracting air. Also known as a **BC** or **BCD** (**Buoyancy Compensation Device**).

Cam Band – The strap that holds the tank to the **BC**.

Cave – A natural feature which has an overhead environment and no direct access to the surface. Cave diving should only be done with specialized training, equipment, and experience.

Cavern – Another natural, overhead environment that restricts direct access to the surface, but from which surface light is still visible. Also requires specialized training.

CESA -- Controlled Emergency Swimming Ascent. Ascending in a controlled manner by swimming, constantly exhaling to avoid a lung overexpansion injury. Used when a diver has run out of air, has no redundant air supply, and cannot get to another diver for assistance.

Charles' Law – A gas law relating to pressure, volume, and temperature. As divers, we are primarily concerned with its effects when filling and storing **SCUBA** tanks. As the temperature of the tank increases, so does that of the air inside. That air begins to expand and increase in pressure. Do not store newly filled tanks in hot car trunks! For every degree the temperature rises, there is a pressure increase of approximately five psi.

CMAS – Confederation Mondiale des Activites Subaquatiques. The oldest **SCUBA** certification agency in the world. **CMAS** is governed by technical councils in each country, where it is decided who will be certified to conduct **CMAS**-approved training courses. The current US training partner for **CMAS** is **Scuba Educators International (SEI Diving)**.

CNS – Central Nervous System.

CNS Hit – When the oxygen partial pressure exceeds a certain level, divers can experience a CNS hit. It is characterized by a seizure during which the regulator is likely to be spit out and the diver may drown. It can come on very suddenly. It is possible to recover the diver if the rescuer or dive buddy can get the **reg** back in at the end of the seizure. It usually occurs when using air with higher oxygen content, such as that used by technical divers. Recreational divers are at extremely low risk of taking a hit using air. The depth at which air exceeds the oxygen partial pressure limit is approximately 218 feet.

Computer (comp for short). A submersible electronic device that keeps track of all dive planning information required by divers. Some computers come with sensors for tracking additional information, such as air pressure or heart rate.

Critter – Any animal in the water. It is often called a "critter dive" when the primary purpose is to see aquatic life.

Cylinder – The proper term for the object used to carry our air supply, the tank.

Dalton's Law – Another gas law that states that the percentages of a gas in a mixture will remain the same regardless of the pressure exerted on that gas. At two atmospheres, we take in twice as many air molecules as at the surface, but the 21% oxygen and 79% nitrogen ratios will stay the same.

DAN -- Divers Alert Network. A non-profit organization providing medical advice, referrals, insurance, and other services to **SCUBA** divers.

Decompression (deco) – The process of allowing the accumulated nitrogen in the body to leave via breathing while gradually reducing pressure on the body.

Decompression Procedures – Special procedures followed when conducting dives requiring mandatory decompression stops. These should never be practiced without specialized training.

Decompression Sickness – A term referring to the symptoms that occur when excess nitrogen comes out of solution and forms bubbles in a diver's blood vessels and soft tissues.

Decompression/Deco Stop – A mandatory stop where the diver must spend a prescribed amount of time before continuing to ascend. There may be multiple stops required, depending on the depth and duration of the dive.

Descent – The process of traveling down into the water column.

Dive Guide -- A relatively new term in the industry, a dive guide is often tasked with leading certified divers on tours underwater. A dive guide may be a professional, or just someone with knowledge of the local sites.

Dive Leader – The individual responsible for some organizational duties when conducting dives or leading other divers. This person may or may not be a professional. This term may not be used in every area.

Divemaster (DM) – A professional rating in the **SCUBA** industry used to designate someone who has elected to pursue a full- or part-time career in teaching others to dive. Each agency has a customized program with different requirements and duties a divemaster may perform.

Dive Safety Officer (DSO) – Used in professional, academic, and military diving operations, the DSO is responsible for every phase of the diving operation. Duties include but are not limited to qualifying divers, setting schedules and planning, safety issues, and emergency management.

Dry Suit – An exposure suit that uses air to insulate the diver and reduce heat loss.

Dump Valve – Found on **BCs** and **lift bags**, this is a spring-loaded valve with a cord, used to vent air in a controlled manner. Commonly found on the shoulder of a BC opposite the power inflator, or on the bottom at the rear.

Enriched Air – Air that has oxygen content greater than 21%. Recreational diving uses mixtures of up to 40% oxygen.

Entry – Any method used to enter the water from shore or a boat.

First Stage – The part of a regulator that reduces the tank pressure to an intermediate pressure and also distributes breathing gas to the various regulator components.

Free Dive -- Also known as skin diving, free diving has grown in popularity over the years. It is also called breath-hold diving as it is performed on one breath.

Full Face Mask (FFM) – A mask that encloses the entire face and incorporates a regulator second stage. Very useful in cold or contaminated water, it does require some special training. It also allows voice communication between divers and the surface with specialized communication equipment.

Gas – Divers frequently refer to their air supply as their gas supply. Gas mixes other than air are used in technical diving, so "gas" is a good generic term for referring to whatever the diver is using.

Gas Laws – Refers to those laws of physics that govern the behavior of various gasses used in diving.

Giant Stride -- A type of entry most often used from a boat or dock. The diver merely takes a big step to enter the water, while looking up and straight ahead.

GUE – **Global Underwater Explorers**. A certification agency.

Helium – An inert gas used by technical divers to reduce the effects of nitrogen narcosis. Helium is found in **trimix**, a breathing gas which can be used only after receiving specialized training.

Henry's Law - A gas law governing and explaining the ability of a liquid under pressure to absorb gas molecules. The greater the pressure, the more gas molecules that can be kept in solution. Once the pressure is released those molecules begin to come out of solution and form bubbles.

HID Light – **High Intensity Discharge Light**. A type of high-power light used in technical diving.

Hood – A neoprene head-covering used to retain heat.

HSA -- **Handicapped Scuba Association**. A certification agency for disabled divers.

IANTD -- **International Association of Nitrox and Technical Divers**. A certification agency.

IDEA -- **International Diving Educators Association**. A certification agency.

Indentured Servitude – See **Internship**.

Insta-Buddy -- Term used to describe the person on the boat or at the site who you don't know, but who will be your new dive buddy. Some boats require every diver to have a buddy and will pair up divers who do not know each other. Careful planning and discussion is often required before getting into the water with such a person, since training and experience is often very different.

Internship – Used in some professional training programs, the internship is a period during which divers who desire to become professionals participate in the training of new divers while being guided by an instructor. Internships vary greatly and careful research is required before signing up for one. They are usually unpaid and may actually require the diver to pay for the *"privilege"* of working for the instructor, shop, or resort.

J Valve – A type of tank valve no longer in common use. The J valves had a feature whereby a rod could be pulled and give the diver an extra 300-500 psi of air. It was then that the diver knew it was time to ascend. One problem is that the rod could be pulled accidentally without the diver knowing it. **SPGs** have replaced the J valve but there are some still in use. Divers should not rely on them unless they are fully aware of the condition and use of the valve.

Jacket BC – A **Buoyancy Compensator** with a **bladder** that wraps around the diver. This is the most common type of **BC** in use at this time.

K Valve – The K valve replaced the **J valve** when **SPGs** began to make their way into mainstream usage. It is called the K valve simply because when the new catalog came out and the valve was put in, it followed the **J valve**. K came after J, and there you go.

LED – **Light Emitting Diode**. The newest entry into the dive light realm. Bright, long lasting, and with low power usage, they are the latest in dive light technology, available in sizes ranging from small flashlights to high-power canister lights.

Lift Bag – A device used to raise sunken objects from the water. Filled with air from the diver's tank or some other supply, lift bags require some training to use safely and effectively.

Light Zone – The area in a wreck or other overhead environment where light from the surface can still be seen and used to navigate out of the overhead area if necessary.

Lubber Line – The line on a diver's compass that is lined up parallel with the diver's body while swimming a course.

Maximum Operating Depth (MOD) – When using enriched air, divers must calculate the MOD of the gas mix they are using, to avoid oxygen toxicity. This depth must not be exceeded on the dive. The higher the oxygen content of the gas, the shallower the MOD due to increases in oxygen partial pressure (**PPO2**).

Mentor – A more experienced diver who guides new divers in the real-world ways that dives are conducted. Mentors encourage and inspire new divers to improve, become safer and more skilled.

Mil – Spoken abbreviation for millimeter. Divers often refer to their wet suits in terms of the thickness of the neoprene, i.e., "My five mil suit."

NACD – **National Association of Cave Diving**. A technical certification agency for cave divers.

NAUI – **National Association of Underwater Instructors**. A certification agency.

Negative – Short for being negatively buoyant, meaning an object that, unassisted, will sink. If you must swim or tread water to keep from descending, you are negative.

Neoprene – A material used to make exposure suits. Neoprene is a type of rubber that has been injected with bubbles of nitrogen to add to the insulation properties of the material.

Neutral – The state of being neither negatively buoyant nor positively buoyant underwater. What every diver should be capable of and striving for.

185

Newbie – Slang for "new diver."

Nitrogen – An inert gas found in nature. The air we breathe is approximately 79% nitrogen.

Nitrox – See **Enriched Air**.

No Decompression Limit (NDL) – The time one may spend at a given depth and theoretically still ascend directly to the surface at a safe rate with minimal risk of decompression sickness. Safety stops are not mandated, but are always recommended.

NSS-CDS – **National Speleological Society-Cave Diving Section**. A technical certification agency for cave diving.

Nudibranch – A type of slug-like sea animal, often beautifully colored. It is also slang for the snot hanging from a diver's nose that is visible to all.

Octopus (octo) -- The diver's alternate second stage regulator.

O-Ring – A ring made up of some type of rubber compound, used to seal mating surfaces.

Overhead Environment – A term used to describe a dive site that has no direct access to the surface. Caves, caverns, wrecks, and ice all fall into this category. Requires special training and experience to dive safely.

Over Pressure Valve (OPV) – A valve used on **BC**s, **Dry Suits**, **Lift Bags**, and **Regulators** to prevent any type of rupture due to high pressures exceeding those recommended for operation of the device.

Oxygen – One of the components of the air we breathe and often used to fill **SCUBA** tanks. Oxygen is 21% of regular air (the balance being nitrogen). **Enriched Air** will have higher percentages of oxygen. It is a common mistake in the media and elsewhere to use the term oxygen when the subject is simple air.

P Valve – A valve installed on a **dry suit** that, in combination with a condom catheter for men and another device known as a **"She P"®** for women, allows a **dry suit** diver to urinate without taking the suit off. It can be used in or out of the water.

PADI – Professional Association of Dive Instructors. A certification agency.

PDIC – Professional Dive Instructors Corporation. A certification agency.

Penetration – A dive on a wreck or into a cave that results in the diver being in an **overhead environment**. Special training is required for dives of this type.

Positive -- Short for being positively buoyant, meaning an object that, unassisted, will float/ascend. If you have difficulty with your initial descent or find yourself drifting upward during a dive, you are positive.

PPO2 – Acronym for oxygen partial pressure.

PSI – Pounds per square inch; a unit of pressure usually expressed in lower case, i.e., psi.

Recreational Limits – The limits for recreational dives. Commonly taken to mean no mandatory **decompression stops**, no **overhead environments**, and for most agencies, a maximum depth of 130 feet. There may be other limits imposed by various agency standards and guidelines.

Reel - A device consisting of some type of **spool** around which line is wound. It is used for navigation in **wrecks**, **caves**, and open water when visibility is poor.

Regulator (reg) – The device that allows us to breath from a **SCUBA** tank.

RMV – Respiratory Minute Volume. A diver's **SAC** rate expressed in volume (cubic feet) rather than pressure (psi).

Rock Bottom -- A method of managing one's air supply as mentioned in Chapter Five. Rock Bottom involves more complicated calculations than are necessary for the average new diver.

RSTC – Recreational SCUBA Training Council. An organization made up of member agencies that voluntarily agree on standards for diver training.

Run Time – Used by some divers to indicate the total length of a dive.

SAC – Acronym for **Surface Air Consumption**.

Safety Sausage – A tall, inflatable tube used at the surface to signal a diver's location when observers are too far away to readily see the diver. Also used from depth with a reel and line, to allow boat crews to track the progress of divers on drift dives.

SCUBA -- **Self Contained Underwater Breathing Apparatus**. The unit consisting of the **BC**, **Regulator**, and **Cylinder** that allows us to explore underwater.

SDI – Scuba Divers International. A certification agency.

SEI Diving – Scuba Educators International. A certification agency.

Semi-Dry Suit -- A **wet suit** with latex seals that is a functional cross between a true **wet suit** and a **dry suit**. The good **semi-dry suit** traps a layer of water next to the diver, where it stays (rather than water flowing through, as happens with **wet suits**).

Skin Diving – Also known as **free diving**, it is the act of diving with a mask, snorkel, fins, and perhaps weights, but no **SCUBA** unit.

Slate -- A hard, plastic surface designed for written communication underwater.

Snorkel -- A tube with a mouthpiece that allows a diver or swimmer to breathe on the surface with their face in the water.

Spool – Like a **reel,** the spool is used for underwater navigation and to shoot **SMBs**, but it has no handle or crank.

SSI -- Scuba Schools International. A certification agency.

Staged Decompression -- The process of off-gassing during a dive that has exceeded the **No Decompression Limits** by using planned stops at regular intervals. It may also require the diver to switch to different gas mixes during the process.

Suit Bottle – A separate air supply (usually about 6 cu ft) used to inflate the diver's **dry suit**.

Surface Air Consumption (SAC) -- The amount of air a diver uses at the surface. Using the formula explained in Chapter Five, divers can estimate the amount of time a tank will last at a given depth.

Surface Marker Buoy (SMB) – Similar to a **lift bag,** the **SMB** is used to mark the position of a diver or object underwater. It is used with a **reel** or **spool** to launch the **SMB** from depth while maintaining position.

Tank -- See **Cylinder.**

TDI -- Technical Diving International. A certification agency.

Technical Dive – Any dive beyond normal recreational limits, often requiring staged decompression. Requires specialized training and equipment.

Technical Diver – Name commonly given to divers who are diving beyond recreational limits, have received specialized training, and who often carry specialized equipment.

Training Dive – A dive conducted for skill-training purposes. It may be overseen by an instructor as part of ongoing education, or it may simply be a dive that the buddy team decides to dedicate to practice of skills.

Trimix – A gas mixture used by technical divers to offset the effects of nitrogen narcosis and nitrogen loading. Trimix is often composed of oxygen, nitrogen, and helium.

Turn Pressure – The term is used in dive planning to denote the tank pressure at which the dive is turned to begin the swim back to the entry point

UTD – Unified Team Diving. A training agency.

Vent – To allow air to escape from a **BC** or **dry suit** by means of a valve, to control buoyancy.

Wet Suit – A type of exposure suit that allows a layer of water between the diver and the suit. The diver's body heats the water and the suit slows the amount of heat loss. Usually made of neoprene.

Wing – The air bladder of a **Back Plate and Wing BC**.

YMCA SCUBA – The first national US certification program. Closed in 2008, it led to the birth of **Scuba Educators International (SEI Diving).**

Appendix B:

Recommended Reading

In my experience as a diver and instructor, I have found it beneficial to use many sources of information. All of the following have contributed a surprising amount to my knowledge base and have improved my diving. Some of the listings below are for training manuals, while others are for books that are fact-based accounts of real divers and events from which we can all learn. I have listed them in rough order of importance, at least in terms of what they have meant to me.

SCUBA Diving 4th Edition (2010) by Dennis Graver, Champaign, Illinois: Human Kinetics.

Diving Fundamentals for Leadership (2007) by Tom Leaird, Muncie, Indiana: Tom Leaird's Underwater Service.

US Navy Diving Manual Rev. 6 (2008) by Supervisor of Diving, United States Navy, US Dept. of the Navy.

NOAA Diving Manual 4th Edition (2001), James T. Joiner, Editor, Flagstaff, Arizona: Best Publishing.

The Tao of Survival Underwater – Expedition and Mixed Gas Diving Encyclopedia (2008) by Tom Mount, Miami Shores, Florida: International Association of Nitrox Divers.

Technical Diver Encyclopedia (2003) by Tom Mount, Miami Shores, Florida: International Association of Nitrox Divers.

The Technical Diving Handbook (1998) by Gary Gentile, Philadelphia, Pennsylvania: Gary Gentile Productions.

Encyclopedia of Recreational Diving (1998-2003), Drew Richardson, Editor, Rancho Santa Margarita, California: PADI.

Oxygen Hacker's Companion (2001, 2007, 2009) by Vance Harlow, Warner, New Hampshire: Airspeed Press.

SCUBA Regulator Maintenance and Repair (1999-2002) by Vance Harlow, Warner, New Hampshire: Airspeed Press.

Regulator Savvy, 1st Edition (2003) by Pete Wolfinger, Greensboro, NC: Scuba Tools Inc.

The DAN Guide to Dive Medical Frequently Asked Questions (2003) by Divers Alert Network, Durham, NC: Divers Alert Network.

The Last Dive (2000) by Bernie Chowdhury, New York, NY: HarperCollins Publishers, Inc.

Shadow Divers (2004) by Robert Kurson, New York, NY: Ballantine Books.

Deep Descent (2001) by Kevin F. Murray, New York, NY: Touchstone.

Fatal Depth (2003, 2004) by Joseph Haberstroh, Guilford, Connecticut: The Lyons Press.

The Great Lakes Diving Guide, 2nd Edition (2008) by Chris Kohl, West Chicago, IL: Seawolf Communications, Inc.

Buckets and Belts (2009) by William Lafferty and Valerie Van Heest, Holland, MI: In-Depth Additions.

* * * * *

There are also a number of websites that I refer to for information and to socialize with other divers. Among them are the following:

The Cyber Diver (www.cyberdiver.com).

The Deco Stop (www.thedecostop.com).

Divers Alert Network (www.DAN.org). Includes online courses, the Annual Accident Report, and answers to questions regarding the Divers Alert Network insurance program.

Grateful Diver's School of Diving (www.nwgratefuldiver.com) has lots of great articles. The gas management article there is more comprehensive than the one in this work and I highly recommend it if you want to expand your knowledge of the subject.

Recreational Scuba Training Council (www.rstc.com). The RSTC establishes standards for many levels of dive training. Their current standards can be found here except for the Open Water Diver Standard, which may be found at www.universoblu.it/Standard_RSTC_per_OpenWaterDiver.pdf

Scubaboard (www.scubaboard.com).

Second Edition Additional Reading Recommendations

The Six Skills (2011) by Steve Lewis, Rosseau, Ontario Canada: SL Publications

Staying Alive: Applying Risk Management to Advanced Scuba Diving (2014) by Steve Lewis, Rosseau, Ontario Canada: SL Publications

INDEX

194

About the Author

Jim Lapenta was first certified as an Open Water Diver through the Professional Association of Diving Instructors (PADI) in 2004. In the next two years, he went on to earn his PADI Divemaster certification, in addition to the specialties of Nitrox, Deep, Wreck, Underwater Navigation, Drysuit, Equipment Specialist, and Rescue Diver. He then earned certifications for Intro to Tech and Helitrox with the National Association of Underwater Instructors (NAUI), followed by crossover training with the YMCA beginning in the fall of 2007. Immediately impressed by the YMCA agency's philosophy, comprehensive training methods, and ethical standards, Jim earned his Instructor certification with them. When the YMCA decided to close the program in 2008, a group of dedicated Instructors concluded that the program had too rich a history and tradition of skills and education to let it be lost. Scuba Educators International was formed as a result, and Jim made the transition to it in October of 2008. He received his Ice Diver certification from SEI Diving in 2009, and his CMAS 2 Star Instructor Rating in August of 2010.

Jim has logged dives in conditions ranging from warm, clear water in the Florida Keys and Bonaire to the cold depths of Lake Erie and the St. Lawrence River. He is happiest when exploring wrecks, but finds magic in the chance to get underwater just about anywhere. A fan and proponent of local diving, he has explored numerous lakes and quarries in West Virginia, Ohio, and Pennsylvania.

As of 2011, Jim has certified or assisted in the certification of over 100 students from Junior Open Water to Divemaster. He specializes in working with younger people and others needing extra attention for any reason. Jim has authored a course in Underwater Navigation for SEI Diving, and developed a new Advanced Open Water course that has drawn students from hundreds of miles away. He has had numerous articles published online, most notably at www.dailyscubadiving.com. For SEI he is also a co-author and editor of the SEI Search and Recovery and Public Safety Diving course.

In 2012 Jim added SDI/TDI Instructor Credentials to his portfolio and now offers both Recreational and Entry Level Technical training to his students. In addition he is an authorized TDI Edge/HOG

Equipment Service Clinic Instructor. In 2014 he is planning to add SDI Solo and OW Sidemount Instructor to his credentials.

About the Editor

Elizabeth Babcock has been writing since someone first put a crayon in her hand, and has been a diver since 2000. She spends her surface intervals in private practice as a psychotherapist for individual clients, in addition to doing a variety of community education seminars and trainings for other healthcare professionals. Elizabeth has written many wellness articles, which you are invited to read at www.elizabethbabcock.com.

About the Illustrator

Casey Peel is a long-time swimmer and began SCUBA training as a result of her work on this book. A budding artist in high school as this book first went to press, she is interested in more work of this type. Inquiries may be directed to the author.

Cover Design by John Stanton   www.gabrielshornpress.com

CPSIA information can be obtained
at www.ICGtesting.com
Printed in the USA
BVHW041157271118
534113BV00017B/125/P

9 781494 900250